The Pentester Blueprint

Starting a Career as an Ethical Hacker

Phillip L. Wylie
Kim Crawley

WILEY

I dedicate The Pentester Blueprint *to my wife Tiffany and daughter Jordan. Without your love and support, this would not have been possible. As always you support me in my endeavors, encouraging me every step of the way.*

—Phillip L. Wylie

To my loving rock musician boyfriend Jason, my stuffed animal family for assuring me of the rest that I need in order to work effectively, and my late father Michael Crawley for encouraging my very early interest in computers and raising me to write for a living.

— Kim Crawley

About the Authors

Phillip L. Wylie is the Lead Curriculum Developer for Point3 Federal, Adjunct Instructor at Dallas College, and The Pwn School Project founder. Phillip has over 23 years of industry experience in disciplines ranging from system administrator, network security engineer, and application security engineer. He has spent the last eight-plus years as a pentester. During his pentesting career, Phillip has performed pentests of networks, wireless networks, and applications, as well as red team operations and social engineering.

Phillip started his career in pentesting as a consultant, where he spent his first five years. These years gave him experience in various environments for Fortune 500 companies in a broad range of industries. Phillip has a passion for mentoring, educating, and helping others. His passion for education and the cybersecurity community motivated him to start teaching and to found The Pwn School Project, a monthly educational meetup focusing on cybersecurity and ethical hacking. His education efforts, however, expanded beyond the classroom and The Pwn School Project. He can be found routinely giving presentations and teaching workshops at cybersecurity conferences.

Phillip teaches Ethical Hacking and Web Application Pentesting at Dallas College in Dallas, TX. Phillip is a co-host for The Uncommon Journey podcast. Phillip has an associate degree in Computer Networking and holds these cybersecurity certifications: CISSP, NSA-IAM, OSCP, and GWAPT. During his system administrator career, Phillip attained these industry certifications; Microsoft MCSE for Windows NT 4.0 and Windows 2000, Novell CNE, and Cisco CCNA.

Kim Crawley is dedicated to researching and writing about a plethora of cybersecurity issues. Some of the companies Kim has worked for over the years include Sophos, AT&T Cybersecurity, BlackBerry Cylance, Tripwire, and Venafi. All matters red team, blue team, and purple team fascinate her. But she's especially fascinated by malware, social engineering, and advanced persistent threats.

Kim's extracurricular activities include running an online cybersecurity event called DisInfoSec and autistic self-advocacy. When she's not working, Kim loves JRPGs (especially the Persona series), trying to cook Japanese and Korean dishes, goth music and fashion, and falling down Wikipedia and TV Tropes rabbit holes.

Acknowledgments

I thank all of my students and the people I have mentored over the years: You helped me realize my passion for teaching. I thank my friend and fellow adjunct instructor Jason Alvarado for hiring me to teach at Dallas College (formerly Richland College). Teaching Ethical Hacking and Web Application Pentesting helped me discover my love for teaching, which has opened so many doors. I thank my friend and Dallas Hackers Association founder Wirefall for your friendship and for founding the Dallas Hackers Association.

The Dallas Hackers Association was pivotal in getting me involved in the hacking and cybersecurity community. This led to speaking and teaching workshops at cybersecurity conferences, where I have connected with so many amazing people. Thanks to Wirefall, I met Marcus Carey, the author of the *Tribe of Hackers* book series (Wiley, 2019). Thanks to Marcus for including me in the *Tribe of Hackers Red Team* book, which has been very helpful in my career and ultimately led to my being offered the opportunity to write this book. I acknowledge Marcus for his contributions to the cybersecurity community and for his efforts for the betterment of our world and for inspiring me to make the world a better place.

Last, but definitively not least, I thank Kim Crawley, my amazing coauthor, who helped me take my conference talk from conception to a book. Thanks for helping me take an idea—28 PowerPoint slides—and breathing life into it.

I would like to thank my friend, Rhea Santos for taking time out of her schedule to create the artwork for the chapters of the book. Rhea is a friend and someone that I have taught and mentored. It is so fitting to have her art in The Pentester Blueprint since it was the people that I taught and mentored that inspired me to write this book.

Thanks also go to Jim Minatel at Wiley for the opportunity to write this book and to Gary Schwartz and the rest of the Wiley staff for making this book a reality. Your hard work is much appreciated.

—Phillip L. Wylie

I'm tremendously grateful to Phillip Wylie for inviting me to collaborate with him on *The Pentester Blueprint*. Phil developed a great Pentester Blueprint curriculum, which he has perfected while teaching it in workshops and schools across the United States. This book brings that curriculum to the masses while adding some of my own ideas. Many, many ethical hackers have been born from Phil's generosity with his expertise! Phil, you've been a pleasure to work with, and I look forward to working with you again on future projects.

I also thank Gary Schwartz for being such a patient editor. This book has benefited greatly from your work behind the scenes. I also enjoyed our funny discussions of popular culture over email.

I thank Jim Minatel, Associate Publisher at Wiley, for also being vital to the success of this book. I really appreciate your encouragement of my work. I shine with the support of publishing professionals like you.

I thank Victoria Lamont, my loving sister and the only blood relative left in my life. Although you say you don't understand my technical jargon, you've been very supportive of my cybersecurity research and writing career. Thank you so much for everything you do!

On that note, I thank my de facto "parents-in-law" Joe and Laurie, and Rose. You always make Christmas special for me. Jason, I look forward to giving you autographed copies of this book.

Thank you Olena, for being such a supportive friend.

I thank Bora's Joe Pettit and David Turner, well-known names in the world of tech marketing. You both took a chance on me and helped to start the career that I enjoy today. I'm eternally grateful, because getting your foot in the door is always the hardest part of establishing a career.

I thank Marcus Carey. Not only did you write an excellent foreword to this book, you also do great work helping people get into the cybersecurity field. I'm doing my best to read all of your books! It was also an honor to be included in your first volume of *Tribe of Hackers*.

Finally, I thank my boyfriend Jason, once again. I listen to your music whenever I miss you, and I always look forward to spending time with you in my apartment or yours, once a week. Your encouragement of me during this successful period of my life is always appreciated. I love you, darling.

— Kim Crawley

Contents at a Glance

Contents

Foreword

I'd say the most coveted positions in cybersecurity and information technology as a whole are roles as penetration testers, or *pentesters*, also known as *ethical hackers*. I want to emphasize the ethical part of that last sentence. There are many that go down the path of self-study, trying to get into the field, who end up crossing the line into unethical and even illegal behavior.

Remember always to use your superpowers for good. Funny enough, when people find out that I'm an ethical hacker, many ask me to break into something for them. They also ask how they can learn what I know so that they can get a cool job. I certainly will point them to two books that I co-authored with Jennifer Jin, *Tribe of Hackers: Cybersecurity Advice from the Best Hackers in the World* and *Tribe of Hackers Red Team: Tribal Knowledge from the Best in Offensive Cybersecurity,* both published by Wiley in 2019, to which my friends Kim Crawley and Phillip Wylie contributed.

If I were to point someone trying to get into this line of work, I'd most certainly point them to Phillip Wylie. Phillip is the only person I know that can teach you how to break into a company ethically for security purposes and to have wrestled a bear and lived to talk about it. Like many of our backgrounds, Phillip's was unique and something that should be embraced. There is no one correct path to be a penetration tester.

Phillip continues to pay it forward by helping tons of people to learn about ethical hacking and volunteering hundreds of hours helping people learn. You will learn a lot from this book, and I'm going to ask you a favor: Please pay it forward and help someone else by teaching them something that you already know or learn from this book which can help them out.

I just want to thank Phillip for being such a blessing to so many people. I hope you learn a lot or even fill in some blanks in your knowledge. I wish you an abundance of success on your journey.

Marcus J. Carey
Creator of Tribe of Hackers Series

Introduction

The Pentester Blueprint was born from ethical hacker Phillip Wylie's excellent pentesting curriculum of the same name. Whether or not you're able to attend one of the many workshops and classes that Phil gives every year, this book will teach you not only how to become a pentester but also how to become a successfully employed pentester! By reading this book, you have started the journey on your ethical hacking career. The future looks bright for you!

How I Became a Pentester

"My journey to becoming a pentester started with my first IT job as a system administrator. In my previous career as a draftsman, I learned about the system administrator role. It intrigued me and seemed more interesting that creating drawings on AutoCAD. I taught myself how to build computers and about a year later I took a certified NetWare engineer (CNE) certification course and learned the Novell NetWare network operating system. Not long after completing the course I got my first system administrator job and spent a little over six years in that IT discipline. I got interested in information security three years into my system administrator career and later moved into a network security role at the company where I worked. One and a half years later I became part of a newly formed two person application security team. I got to learn how to use web application vulnerability scanners and learned about penetration testing, which became my next career move. Almost seven years later I was part of a layoff and was fortunate enough to land my first penetration testing job working as a consultant for a cyber security consulting company. That was the start of my eight and a half penetration testing career."

Who Should Read This Book

This book is for individuals of all ages who are considering a career in the pentesting field. All genders and walks of life can appreciate this book, as long as you can develop the hacker mindset! Of course, we will explain that mindset to you and help you out every step of the way. Whether you already work in IT or you haven't worked with computers professionally before, we've done our best to make our ideas accessible to you.

What You Will Learn

Pentesting requires not only computer technology skill but also practical thinking. Most of your work will be with computers and their networks, but not all of it! Pretending to be a con artist and lockpicking can also be useful skills for an ethical hacker, as malicious cyberattackers also fool human beings and physically penetrate buildings.

We'll teach you how to do some of that cool Hollywood hacking stuff for real, but only with consenting targets. Most importantly, we'll also show you how you can get hired to do that sort of work!

We share our expertise, but we also made sure to get ideas from many other gainfully employed pentesters in this book. You will benefit from our wide range of experiences and what we've learned while being "good hackers" in real life.

How This Book Is Organized

We strongly recommend that you read this book in a linear fashion, because each new chapter builds upon the previous chapter.

Chapter 1: What Is a Pentester? In this chapter, we introduce you to the concept of pentesting. Why do companies need pentests? How will your work help to improve your clients' security? There are also different types of pentesting, which we will summarize within this chapter.

Chapter 2: Prerequisite Skills Here we explain the computer technical skills that you'll need before you focus on learning ethical hacking skills. These skills pertain to operating systems and computer networking. We also explain a wide range of cybersecurity concepts. All areas of cybersecurity are interconnected, so understanding them is essential.

Chapter 3: Education of a Hacker In this chapter, we explain the general ethical hacking skills that you'll need in your pentesting career. We also introduce the hacker mindset and the Pentester Blueprint Formula!

Chapter 4: Education Resources Next we explain how you can continue to learn about pentesting after you've read this book. We recommend specific books and training programs. The pentesting lab you'll build in the next chapter also helps.

Chapter 5: Building a Pentesting Lab Here we explain how you can build your very own pentesting lab, both in the comfort of your own home and in forms that you can take with you on the go. We'll explain how to simulate hacking systems and targets.

Chapter 6: Certifications and Degrees There are many certifications and resources available that can help you become an employed pentester. We'll explain which ones are the most important in this chapter.

Chapter 7: Developing a Plan Here we will help you analyze which skills you already have and figure out those skills that you'll need to acquire.

Chapter 8: Gaining Experience Getting a job can be a chicken-and-egg problem. You can't get a job without experience, and you can't get experience without a job! We'll explain how you can avoid that trap.

Chapter 9: Getting Employed as a Pentester Now that you have some ethical hacking experience, we'll show you how to become employed as a pentester.

How to Contact the Authors

You can find Phillip Wylie online at:

LinkedIn: www.linkedin.com/in/phillipwylie
Twitter: twitter.com/PhillipWylie

You can find Kim Crawley online at:

LinkedIn: www.linkedin.com/in/kimcrawley
Twitter: twitter.com/kim_crawley

If you believe you have found an error in this book, and it is not listed on the book's page at www.wiley.com, you can report the issue to our customer technical support team at support.wiley.com.

1 What Is a Pentester?

What is a pentester? Although the term may have you thinking of someone who works in quality assurance for an ink pen manufacturing plant, it's actually short for "penetration tester." Pentesters are commonly known as *ethical hackers*.

When you think of the term penetration tester, it makes more sense when you think about someone trying to penetrate the security of a computer, a network, the building in which a network is located, or a website. While the term ethical hacker is a little easier to understand, people are surprised to hear that such a job exists. *Pentesters* assess the security of computers, networks, and websites by looking for and exploiting vulnerabilities–commonly known as *hacking*.

To be clear, not all hackers are bad. Nevertheless, the terms hacker and hacking have been vilified for many years. Ethical hackers use their skills for good to help uncover vulnerabilities that could be exploited by malicious hackers.

The hackers you hear about in the news who are committing crimes should be labeled as cyber criminals. While they are using hacking to commit illegal activities, the intent and purpose of their efforts should be distinguished from pentesting, which is a way to see how cyberattackers can exploit a network for the benefit of security.

Before we get further into the topic, consider the wisdom of a particular philosopher:

> *With great power comes great responsibility.*
>
> *François Voltaire*

You will need permission to hack; otherwise, it would be considered illegal. This quote is a good way to ingrain that message. Prior to starting a pentest, written permission must be obtained.

Synonymous Terms and Types of Hackers

Various terms are synonymous with pentesters and malicious hackers, and we will discuss them to help you understand what each means. The following terms are often used interchangeably and are useful to know.

The most common types of hackers are known as white hat, gray hat, and black hat hackers. These terms were taken from old westerns, where hats were used as a descriptor to tell the good guys from the bad guys:

White hat hackers Ethical hackers (aka pentesters).

Gray hat hackers: Gray hats fall into a fuzzy area. Their intent is not always malicious, but it is not always ethical either.

Black hat hackers: Their intent and purpose are illegal. Cyber criminals fall into this category.

Other commonly used terms for pentesting and pentesters include ethical hackers, offensive security, and adversarial security.

Pentesters are sometimes referred to as the *red team*, and defensive security is referred to as the *blue team*. Although red team is used for offensive security in general, true red teams perform adversarial simulation to emulate malicious hackers and test the blue team. Sometimes companies will also have a purple team. Mix red and blue and you get purple! A *purple team* is simply a small group of people who help to facilitate communication between the red team and blue team. The red team finds vulnerabilities and exploits, and the blue team uses the red team's findings to security harden their networks.

There are also commonly used terms for malicious hackers. Out of respect for good hackers, it is advised that you use these terms rather than the generic term "hacker":

- Threat actor
- Cyber criminals
- Black hat hackers, or black hats for short

Another way that hacking is used is through *hacktivism*. *Hacktivists* are activists that use their hacking skills to support social change, human rights, freedom of speech, or environmental causes. These are still cyberattacks. Even though the hacktivists' motivation may be to help a good cause, these activities are still illegal.

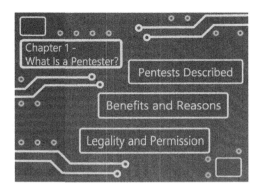

Pentests Described

Pentests assess security from an adversarial perspective. This type of security assessment is the only way to uncover exploitable vulnerabilities and understand their risks. Vulnerability scanning alone or running an application to find vulnerabilities in targeted computers and devices only detects limited vulnerabilities, and by successfully exploiting or hacking the discovered vulnerabilities, it is possible to find ones that would have otherwise gone undetected.

This approach to security testing allows pentesters to mimic a malicious hacker in order to traverse the complex layers of systems to detect vulnerabilities beneath the surface. A vulnerability scan alone misses exploitable security flaws that are only visible on the surface of the system. Getting past the initial system layer allows you to assess security to see how far an attacker could get into your system, or to see if the possibility exists to access and compromise other systems or networks.

Pentesters use similar, or sometimes the same, tactics, techniques, and procedures (TTPs) as are used by cyber criminals. The emulation of an adversary can vary with the type and scope of a test, which we will cover in greater depth in the sections that follow. Pentests are performed on a variety of computers and networking devices. As humans are often fooled in order to conduct cyberattacks, sometimes you may be asked to test them as well. As technology evolves, newer technologies can become targets for testing. Too seldom, security is an afterthought when it should be considered up-front in the design phase.

Benefits and Reasons

The benefits and reasons for conducting pentests have become more recognized by private- and public-sector organizations, and the need to conduct them continues to grow. A decade ago, pentests were typically performed by consultants or contractors. Most companies did not employ their own pentesters, but as the need increased, more companies built their own pentesting teams.

The benefit of pentesting is that it provides a view of the security posture from an adversary's point of view. As we discussed, the best way to understand how an adversary sees security is to have a pentest performed.

Some of the most common reasons for pentests are as follows:

- Discovering and remediating vulnerabilities in order to mitigate possible breaches.
- Regulatory compliance is a major driver for companies to conduct pentests. Of course, this should not be the only reason—security should be the main purpose. Nonetheless, Payment Card Industry-Data Security Standard (PCI-DSS) and General Data Protection Regulation (GDPR) are two major regulations. They pertain to payment systems ranging from those seen in brick-and-mortar stores to those implemented in ecommerce.

Knowledge of pentesting techniques is helpful to more than just pentesters. Understanding how malicious hackers think, as well as the TTPs used by cyber criminals, are helpful to defenders in all areas of information security.

Some areas that can benefit from an understanding of pentesting are as follows:

- Security operations center (SOC) analysts
- Network security analysts and engineers
- Digital forensics and incident response (DFIR)
- Purple teams (a collaboration of defensive and offensive security)
- Application security

SOC analysts and network security personnel can better understand malicious network traffic with pentesting knowledge. DFIR investigators benefit from understanding cyberattacks, which can be learned from pentesting. Purple teams attack and defend digital assets, so pentesting knowledge is essential. Pentesting is useful for application security analysts, and it can be used to assess and secure applications. Knowledge of pentesting is useful throughout all areas of information security. This knowledge is helpful in defending networks, computing platforms, applications, and other technology assets. Understanding pentesting is useful for those working with pentesters. An educated consumer can better select consultants or contractors to conduct pentests or to hire permanent staff for pentesting.

Legality and Permission

Hacking is illegal without permission, so getting written permission prior to starting a pentest is absolutely necessary. Without it, if the pentest causes an outage or damage to a system, it could lead to legal problems. Without written permission, it's the pentester's word against the client's.

The *statement of work* (*SOW*) should include verbiage giving pentesters permission to perform the pentest. It is important that the pentest adhere to a well-defined scope in order to prevent legal problems and customer dissatisfaction. Such permission can also include a document referred to as a *get-out-of-jail-free card*, which can offer legal protection if you make certain mistakes within the scope defined by the SOW. This is especially necessary when performing pentests against buildings, as it may be useful when being questioned by building security or law enforcement.

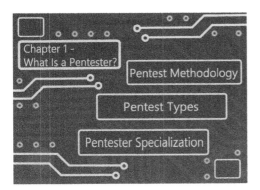

Pentest Methodology

A methodology is required in order to provide consistent and thorough pentests. A pentest methodology ensures that all of the steps were completed during a pentest. A *pentest methodology* is a repeatable process that other pentesters on a team can duplicate to deliver consistent quality. Methodologies are especially important when training new pentesters, giving them a checklist to follow that helps them make sure that they complete all of the required steps in a pentest.

The following list contains some common industry-recognized pentesting methodologies:

Penetration Testing Execution Standard (PTES): `www.pentest-standard.org`

Open Source Security Testing Methodology Manual (OSSTMM): `www.isecom.org/OSSTMM.3.pdf`

NIST 800-115 (National Institute of Standards and Technology): `csrc.nist.gov/publications/detail/sp/800-115/final`

OWASP Testing Guide (Open Web Application Security Project): `www.owasp.org/images/1/19/OTGv4.pdf`

Of the pentest methodologies listed here, the *OWASP Testing Guide* focuses on web application pentests and is the industry standard for those types of pentests. The first three methods are widely used and referenced in books and courses, and some organizations use a combination of these methodologies. Pentest reports and SOWs often document the methodology and the tools used during pentests.

The *Penetration Testing Execution Standard (PTES)* contains the seven main sections of a pentest, which cover all of the required steps of a pentest. Not only does the PTES offer a comprehensive methodology, but PTES offers technical guidelines at `www.pentest-standard.org/index.php/PTES_Technical_Guidelines`.

The PTES technical guidelines detail procedures to follow during a pentest. The guidelines are a good reference for tools, resources, and tasks. We will go into more detail of the PTES methodology, since it is the most commonly used one. PTES is the result of a collaboration of some of the most respected and knowledgeable information security practitioners in the industry.

The seven sections of the PTES are as follows:

1. Pre-engagement Interactions
2. Intelligence Gathering
3. Threat Modeling
4. Vulnerability Analysis
5. Exploitation
6. Post Exploitation
7. Reporting

These are summarized in the following sections. For more detail, see the PTES website at `www.pentest-standard.org`.

Pre-engagement Interactions

This is the planning phase, and it introduces the tools and techniques to be used during the pentests. The scope of a pentest is defined during this phase, as well as the cost, beginning and ending times, and allowed testing times. Pentesting has the potential to cause outages, so testing times need to be agreed upon with the client, and the hours for testing and start and end dates for the pentest should be included in the SOW. Questionnaires are used to help define the scope of the pentest and to plan it. The goals of the pentest should be discussed during this phase, and understanding them is helpful in scoping a successful pentest. The rules of engagement should be determined, which define how the pentest is to be done.

Intelligence Gathering

In this phase, intelligence is gathered on targets to discover vulnerabilities and information that can be used to exploit the target. Information like operating system (OS) and software versions are useful in determining if a target is vulnerable and exploitable. Other types of intelligence gathering could require finding out information about individuals, companies, and organizations through the Internet. Intelligence gathering is also referred to as *reconnaissance* and *Open Source Intelligence (OSINT)*.

Threat Modeling

Threat modeling is a process by which potential threats, such as software or OS vulnerabilities, can be identified, enumerated, and prioritized—all from a hypothetical attacker's point of view. The purpose of threat modeling in pentesting is to provide a systematic analysis of the probable attacker's profile, the most likely attack vectors, and the assets most desired by an attacker. This information is used to attack the target. Threat modeling is especially important on more complex targets, and can be more difficult and time-consuming.

Vulnerability Analysis

Vulnerability analysis is the process of discovering flaws in systems and applications that can be leveraged by an attacker. These flaws can range anywhere from host and service misconfiguration to insecure application design. Tools such as port and service scanners and vulnerability scanners are used to discover vulnerabilities. The discovered vulnerabilities are validated to ensure that they are truly vulnerable and not false positives, and then analyzed to verify if they can be exploited. Note that not all vulnerabilities are exploitable, but they should be included in the report. Vulnerabilities that are not exploitable at the time of the pentest could exploited later if an exploit is developed.

Exploitation

This phase of a pentest focuses solely on hacking vulnerable systems detected during the vulnerability analysis phase of the pentest. There are many different things that you could do in this phase, which will depend on what you're testing, and the scope defined in your SOW. It can include using vulnerability scanners, attempting attacks on web applications, trying to access areas of buildings where outsiders aren't permitted, trying to fool human beings, and various other activities that may be attempted by real cyberattackers. Occasionally, you may have to use your imagination, but be sure only to try what is allowed according to your contract! Chapter 5, "Building a Pentesting Lab," will explain the many actions you'll take in this phase in much greater detail.

Post Exploitation

The purpose of this phase is to determine the *value* of the compromised system and to maintain control for later use. The value of the system is determined by the sensitivity of the data stored on it and its usefulness in further exploiting other systems.

Reporting

This phase of the pentest is where the results and findings are documented. The *pentest report* should have an executive summary where the results are communicated in language that can be understood by nontechnical staff. This section of the report is important for explaining the results to management and the various business lines of the organization. Information on vulnerabilities should be documented, reporting on systems that were exploitable and providing details and evidence of the exploitation. Screenshots and ample evidence should be provided to show proof of the vulnerabilities and exploited systems. Recommendations and remediation information, as well as risk ratings for vulnerabilities, should also be contained in the report.

Pentest Types

When a pentest is performed, pentesters are provided with information on the targets that they are testing. This target knowledge can range from minimal information to a great deal of information. You might know absolutely nothing about the system that you're testing, or you might be as familiar with your target as a network administrator! Three main categories define the depth of information provided:

Black box: The target knowledge for this type of pentest is very limited. For a web application, it is typically just the URL of the application. In the case of a network pentest, it can be an IP address or list of IP addresses. In some cases, the pentester may only know the company name, and it is up to the pentester to use reconnaissance to discover IP addresses or URLs to assess. Black box pentests mimic a malicious hacker more than the other methods.

White box: Also referred to as a *crystal box* pentest, in this type of pentest, the pentester is provided with a lot of detailed information on the target being tested. This information can include documents, diagrams, and the user credentials of different user permissions levels. You want to make sure that a normal user of the application cannot access administrative functions.

Gray box: This type of target knowledge falls between black box and white box testing. Gray box pentests are the most common type of the three. The amount of knowledge that you'll have could be anywhere between the extremes of the ignorance of an outsider up to the familiarity of a network administrator. For instance, you might start with as much knowledge of the network as a company insider who doesn't work in the IT department.

Time can be a factor in deciding between black box, white box, and gray box pentests. The more information the pentester has about the target, the more thoroughly the target can be assessed, so this situation is where a white box pentest would be selected. White box pentests also decrease the time needed to perform a pentest. The less knowledge of the target, the longer the testing time required. The black box pentest requires more reconnaissance, which can add to the amount of time needed to perform the pentest. Gray box pentests are in the middle of the two other methods. Web applications are a type of target that benefit from white box pentests because so many of their vulnerabilities exist in their backends, which aren't obvious from the frontends you see in your web browser.

Vulnerability Scanning

Vulnerability scanning is often part of a pentest, but it is not required. Pentesters can manually discover vulnerabilities without using a vulnerability scanner. Vulnerability scanning is often a job role in a threat and vulnerability management program. *Vulnerability scanners* are used to detect specific vulnerabilities that are publicly known and for which programmers have developed tests, and can help speed up the vulnerability discovery process. Scheduled recurring vulnerability scanning should be part of a threat and vulnerability management program. Vulnerability scanners are an important tool in a pentester's toolbox, and one of the first steps in a pentest. Following are some common vulnerability scanners:

- *Nessus* (www.tenable.com/products/nessus) is a vulnerability scanner by Tenable.
- *Nexpose* (www.rapid7.com/products/nexpose) is a vulnerability scanner offered by Rapid7, the creators of the Metasploit exploitation tool.
- *Openvas* (www.openvas.org) is a vulnerability scanner by Greenbone Networks, which offers a free and commercial version of Openvas.
- *Qualys* (www.qualys.com) offers a VMDR cloud-based vulnerability scanner. It's sold through paid subscription, and it is efficient to use, as Qualys's own cloud handles the computing load.

Vulnerability Assessments

Pentests are a type of security assessment, and so are security vulnerability assessments. Sometimes, security vulnerability assessments are requested instead of pentests in order to reduce the risk of a system outage. All of the steps of a pentest are completed except for exploitation (aka hacking). Security vulnerability assessments are a good starting place for junior or entry-level pentesters.

SECURITY VULNERABILITY ASSESSMENT EXAMPLE

One example where a vulnerability assessment was favored over a pentest occurred when I was doing a Wi-Fi pentest for a hospital. The client expressed concern about Wi-Fi-connected medical devices, fearing that an outage or disruption could endanger the health of their patients. Thus, a security vulnerability assessment with a Wi-Fi controller security configuration review was performed instead of a pentest.

Pentest Targets and Specializations

Numerous technologies should be considered when conducting pentests. Technology is constantly evolving and creating new opportunities for threat actors to exploit and gain access to systems and the information that they store. Targets may benefit from general pentesting. Some pentesters work in a variety of areas, and some choose to specialize. Some areas where a pentester can specialize are as follows:

Generalist (network, Wi-Fi, and light web app)

Application (web app, mobile, thick client, and cloud)

Internet of Things (IoT)

Industrial Control Systems (ICS)

Hardware (including medical devices)

Social engineering (people)

Physical (buildings)

Transportation (vehicles, airplanes)

Red team (adversarial simulation)

Generalist Pentesting

Generalist pentesting is a nonspecific category. Generalists perform pentests on local area networks, and Wi-Fi networks and do some light web application pentesting. You can compare a generalist to a general practitioner in the medical field who practices in multiple areas but does not specialize in one specific area. Pentesters commonly start out as generalists, and individuals with an IT or system administrator background are typically a good fit in this category.

Application Pentesting

Application pentesting includes thick client applications, web applications, mobile applications, and cloud applications. Thick client applications are the older application types mentioned in this section. They have been around for many years and are still widely used. Thick client applications are traditionally standalone applications, which don't require Internet access like web applications, nor do they have to connect to other components residing on servers. Thick client applications can be designed to connect to remotely hosted databases or other networked components using a client-server configuration.

Many of the applications that people use every day fall into this category, such as command lines, older versions of productivity software like the Microsoft Office suite, some of the integrated development environments used by computer programmers, and virtual machine clients, such as Oracle VirtualBox. As time goes on, however, fewer and fewer applications fall into this category, as vendors like Microsoft and Adobe see cloud-based Software-as-a-Service (SaaS) as the way to go.

Some applications can fall into multiple categories such as web applications, mobile applications, and cloud-based applications. Applications that are web-based are accessible across different OSes and device types. These applications can be accessed by mobile devices and computers. This is a great area for people with a software development background or application security background.

Internet of Things (IoT)

According to Merriam-Webster Dictionary, the *Internet of Things (IoT)* is:

> *A system of interrelated computing devices, mechanical and digital machines, objects, animals or people that are provided with unique identifiers and the ability to transfer data over a network without requiring human-to-human or human-to-computer interaction.*

IoT can be used to monitor temperature and other conditions of an environment or systems. It can also be used to track inventory and shipping containers, to name some of IoT's functions. It is important to pentest IoT devices in order to prevent data breaches.

Industrial Control Systems (ICS)

Industrial control systems (ICS) are a similar technology to IoT, but they are used to manage industrial equipment including supervisory control and data acquisition (SCADA) and control systems for water treatment facilities and energy production plants. These systems are critical to the operation of cities, power plants, and manufacturing facilities. The safety of people could be compromised if breached, so this makes pentesting these systems crucial.

Hardware and Medical Devices

Hardware and medical devices need to be assessed for security vulnerabilities, so pentests should be performed on these types of technologies. Hardware includes in this category in network devices, such as routers and switches, and medical devices. Medical device security is critical because it could adversely affect a patient's health or risk their life if compromised by a malicious actor. This category has some crossover to IoT.

Social Engineering

Social engineering is a type of security assessment that targets the human element. Very secure systems can be circumvented by hacking or social engineering of people. Social engineering leverages the use of phishing emails to collect information, or user credentials, or deliver malware to collect information, log keystrokes, or remotely control the victim's computer.

Keystroke loggers collect keystrokes entered by victims. The keystrokes can contain sensitive information and usernames and passwords. Social engineering also makes use of *vishing*, which is social engineering by calling the target on a telephone. *SMSishing* makes use of SMS by using text messages to socially engineer a target. Social engineers also use USB drives and CDs loaded with malware to exploit computers when the media is inserted into the victim's computer.

Physical Pentesting

Physical pentests target buildings and all types of facilities. If the facility is breached, this puts people and information at risk. If threat actors can bypass physical controls, they have a better chance at getting physical access to computers or servers, and physical access to these systems puts them at higher jeopardy of exploitation. Due to the potential risks, it is critical to pentest physical security.

Transportation Pentesting

Transportation pentesting involves trains, airplanes, cars, buses, and trucks, including self-driven vehicles (also known as *autonomous vehicles*). If compromised, autonomous vehicles could be weaponized to do harm to people if successfully exploited by malicious actors. This makes this another critical technology to pentest.

Red Team Pentesting

Red team pentesting, also known as *adversarial simulation*, mimics threat actors. This type of pentesting is performed in the same way that a malicious hacker or threat actor would attempt to attack a target. Red team assessments test the defenders, and typically the assessment is unannounced to the security staff and incident response (IR) personnel. These types of security assessments not only help uncover vulnerabilities, but they also test the detection, time to detect, and the response by security staff. As Wirefall, Dallas Hackers Association founder says, "The red team tests the blue team." The *blue team* is a common term used for information security personnel—the defenders.

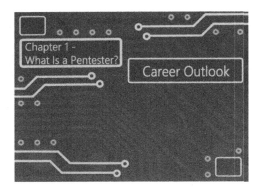

Career Outlook

Just like other areas in information security, there are a lot of opportunities in pentesting. Although pentesting is not a new area, the need has increased, and more companies are starting their own internal pentest teams.

When I started my first pentest assignment in 2012, most of the work was in consulting or contract jobs. Compliance requirements, such as Payment Card Industry–Data Security Standard (PCI-DSS) and the privacy-related compliance requirements of General Data Protection Regulation (GDPR) in the European Union (EU) and California Consumer Privacy Act (CCPA), have increased the need for pentesting. Hiring consultants can be expensive when you have a large number of pentests to be done, so it can be more cost effective to have an internal pentest team. Nonetheless, some companies that have their own pentest teams will still use consultants and contractors, just in case their insiders lose the perspective of an external cyberattacker.

The need for pentesters will continue to grow, especially since not every company currently has its own pentest team in place, and this is a new addition to most information security programs. Pentester roles in some companies might not be a dedicated function, but a rather a subset of the overall duties of information security analysts and engineers.

Other areas of information security where pentesting skills and knowledge are useful include the following:

- SOC (security operations center) analysts
- DFIR (digital forensics and incident response)
- Network security analysts and engineers
- Red team and blue team working collaboratively, with or without a purple team
- Application security
- Security researchers

The skills and knowledge of pentesters helps security professionals better understand an attacker's point of view, equipping them to better detect and defend against malicious activities. This knowledge is helpful to DFIR analysts who need to respond to and investigate incidents. Purple team collaborations between the red team and blue team help tune detection and protection systems including intrusion detection systems (IDS), intrusion prevention systems (IPS), and endpoint detection and response (EDR) systems. Application security professionals can better defend applications with this knowledge and use their pentesting skills to test applications for vulnerabilities. Security researchers range from crowdsourced researchers who work on bug bounty programs to those who work for companies testing the security of products including software, hardware, and vehicles.

Summary

Penetration testing can be an exciting career choice! As more and more of our everyday lives become controlled by computer technology, the demand for pentesters will only increase. A pentester, otherwise known as an *ethical hacker*, simulates cyberattacks so that organizations can learn how to security harden their networks. You could be pentesting specific applications, computers, IoT and network devices, physical buildings, and the people who work for an organization.

You will need to have a detailed agreement with the organization for which you're working that describes what you're allowed to do and what you're not allowed to do when you pretend to be a cyberattacker. Working within that defined scope is absolutely necessary because security testing without the permission of the subject is cyberattacking regardless of your intent!

Different types of pentesting are categorized according to how much knowledge you have of the targeted network before you test. Black box pentesting starts with complete ignorance of how a network is implemented, which is the perspective of an outside cyberattacker. White box pentesting is conducted with detailed knowledge of the target, akin to a network administrator. Gray box testing falls somewhere in between; the perspective of an employee outside the IT department may be equivalent.

There's a lot you'll need to learn before you acquire your first pentesting job. Before you focus your efforts on studying pentesting specifically, you'll need to have an excellent understanding of how computers and networks work. General cybersecurity knowledge is also essential.

In the next chapter, we'll explore what these prerequisites are in order to start your pentesting journey on the right foot.

2

Prerequisite Skills

O ne of the main reasons for writing this book is to share our experience and opinions on what it takes to become a pentester. The concept of this book evolved from an ethical hacking class lecture, to a conference presentation, and now to a book. One topic that was missing at those conferences, and in the available books, was how to become a pentester. You can find lots of books and conference presentations on pentesting, but not on what exactly is required to prepare for a career as a pentester.

Before you start learning how to hack, which is a major piece of the puzzle (though certainly not the only requirement), other prerequisites are required before you start down the path to becoming a pentester. Actually, the starting point is going to be different from person to person. If you are working in information technology (IT), software development, or information security, your prerequisites will vary.

To assess the security of a target and to hack into it, you will need to understand the technology and the security. Deep knowledge of your target is required to be successful at penetrating the target. You don't have to know everything about every technology, but a good understanding is required. If you get command-line access to a Windows or Linux server and you don't know the commands for those operating systems, it is going to limit your success, or at least slow you down.

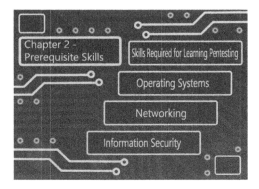

Skills Required for Learning Pentesting

A lot of different technologies are out there in the wild, and it can take time to learn them sufficiently. You are not required to know everything regarding technology to be a pentester, but you need to know the basics, as having a good basic understanding will allow you to learn about new technologies as they are released. Understanding OSs, including Windows and Linux, and networking is "must-have" knowledge to get started and to build upon.

Operating Systems

An *operating system (OS)* is required for the operation of systems including computers, servers, network devices, and mobile devices, such as mobile phones and tablets. Windows and Linux are two of the most widely used operating systems.

Linux is a UNIX-like OS that is widely used on the Internet, mobile devices, and network hardware. IoT devices use Linux as an OS. Several different versions of Linux are available, known as *Linux distributions*, or "distros." Linux is a popular pentesting OS, with Kali Linux and Parrot OS being two of the most common versions in use for pentesting. System administrator–level skills in these OSs should be your goal.

Here are some common Linux distributions:

- Debian
- Ubuntu
- Red Hat Linux
- CentOS
- Arch Linux
- Mint

Windows is the most frequently used desktop OS, and it's very commonly used for servers in businesses large and small. Windows environments can get very complex. Active Directory (AD) makes user and security administration more manageable, especially in large IT environments. AD knowledge is an important component in learning Windows and the Windows networking OS. Start out by learning the Windows OS and then advance to AD. System administrator–level knowledge will give you the skills that you need to pentest Windows environments, and being able to exploit AD accounts can give you access to multiple computers and servers.

System administrator, or sysadmin, skills for Windows and Linux should be your goal. Sysadmins don't rely on a graphical user interface (GUI) to manage systems, but they know how to use it. As a pentester it is important to have the ability to access and manipulate systems from the command line since initial access to the system may only be available at the command line or through a terminal.

Firewalls can be shut down from the command line if the pentester has the necessary security permissions. Also, network settings and other system functions can be changed from the command line. Pentesters can run scripts from the command line. Python, Perl, and Ruby are common languages on Linux systems, and they can be used on Windows as well. Windows PowerShell scripts are very powerful for administering and pentesting Windows-based systems. System configuration mistakes, including network, OS, and software, are a major threat vector exploited by malicious actors, and understanding them will help you as a pentester.

Networking

Websites, IoT, and mobile devices make up our modern, connected world. Included in IoT are your connected home devices and devices used to monitor and track commercial applications. Cellular networks connect mobile phones and devices where phone and data communication lines are not available. Networks, both wired and wireless, provide a threat vector that can be exploited by threat actors to access devices and sensitive information, so it is important that networks be assessed. Pentesters use attacker techniques, and therefore networking skills are required.

Information Security

Pentesters need to understand security, and this skill is needed to be successful as a pentester. This is part of the basic prerequisites for your job. To hack a system, you need to understand the technology of the target as well as the security. Weak security configurations are one of the main reasons why systems get hacked.

Prerequisites Learning

It is important to learn prerequisite skills prior to learning about pentesting. Your time will be well spent, and it will pay off when you start to learn pentesting techniques and throughout your pentesting career. There are a lot of learning options, but following is a quick guide using CompTIA certification-based learning resources as an example.

A+

A+ is a good starting point for your base technology knowledge. A+ covers OSs for mobile devices to computer OSs including Windows, MacOS, Linux, and Android. It also covers hardware, basic IT infrastructure, and networking.

Network+

Network+ teaches routers and switches in the network hardware device coverage. Network+ covers network protocols, standards, and security, as well as network virtualization.

Linux+

Linux+ covers Linux administration for computers, servers, web applications, and mobile devices. Linux+ covers some of the most commonly used Linux distributions.

Security+

Security+ focuses on techniques in risk management, risk mitigation, threat management, and intrusion detection. Security+ covers IT auditor and pentester job roles in addition to system administrator, network administrator, and security administrator roles.

While other resources can be used, the CompTIA-based resources give you an idea of what you need to study to obtain the prerequisites needed by aspiring pentesters. A good resource for videos containing CompTIA learning content is professormesser.com. The videos are free, widely used, and highly recommended for studying for the CompTIA certifications.

Information Security Basics

Pentesting is a process that aids in improving information security. By finding vulnerabilities of all kinds in software, hardware, and networking devices, you can patch, remove, or mitigate these weaknesses. It will definitely help you to become a more effective pentester if you acquire a good general understanding of information security.

Information security is a huge area of study. There are so many concepts and ideas to cover that they can't possibly all be explained within a book chapter. Here we'll summarize some of the basics of information security in order to provide some context for your journey to becoming an ethical hacker. With these concepts in mind, everything else you'll learn about information security will fall into place!

What Is Information Security?

Information security is the process of protecting information. As renowned computer security expert Bruce Schneier always says, "Security is a process, not a product."

What does Schneier mean by that? He means that keeping information secure isn't a matter of just setting up a data system in a secure way, buying some security products, and then forgetting about it. Information security requires constant attention.

As a pentester, you're part of that information security process. You will visit computer networks, both physically and through the Internet, to see what you can penetrate. The discoveries you'll make will be used to improve the security of that computer network. Then, when a year has passed or the computer network changes its configuration or implementation in some significant way, such as when operating systems are upgraded or new network segments are added, you'll perform a penetration test on that computer network again.

People who work in security operations centers, network administrators, blue teamers, and the like will constantly work on the information security process, too. They'll watch real cyberattacks, try to stop them, and recover from the damage. They'll watch the use of their computer networks and make sure that the activity in them is information secure. They'll check to make sure that their computer networks comply with industry-specific and general data security regulations. Whether you're on the red team, blue team, or purple team, or work in any role within the IT department, information security is something that you'll be working on every day.

One popular misconception is that information security only pertains to computer data. But the word "information" is a broad term. Words printed on paper and messages people speak to each other the old-fashioned way also constitute information! Therefore, paper shredders are an information security tool. If people are talking about sensitive information while in the same room together, making sure that there are no unauthorized recording devices lying around is an information security procedure.

Some words and phrases are used interchangeably with information security.

Computer security is information security pertaining specifically to computer data. Cybersecurity means exactly the same thing as computer security. The "cyber" prefix simply means "computer." Network security pertains to securing the data in networks.

So, to sum up, securing data that's being transmitted through a computer network involves network security, cybersecurity, and information security. Securing data that's on an external hard drive that's never connected to a network isn't network security, but it is both cybersecurity and information security. Putting an old printed tax return with sensitive financial and government identification numbers through a paper shredder is information security, but it isn't cybersecurity or network security. That's simple to understand, right?

The CIA Triad

The most fundamental concept in information security is the CIA triad. No, this has nothing to do with the Central Intelligence Agency. The CIA triad stands for *confidentiality*, *integrity*, and *availability*. All information security vulnerabilities, exploits, and attacks pertain to one or more of the three components of this triad.

Confidentiality is making sure that data is only accessible to authorized parties. When sensitive data is exposed to a data breach, that's a threat to confidentiality. If an external cyberattacker penetrates my home PC and looks at the contents of my hard drive, that too is a threat to confidentiality. *Encryption* is the act of rendering information into ciphertext so that only authorized parties can read, or decipher, the information.

Cryptography is a major way that the confidentiality of data is protected. Cyberattackers will occasionally try to attack the ciphers that are used in cryptography, which represent the mathematical code for rendering data as ciphertext. However, cryptography has become increasingly sophisticated and complex over the years, and some ciphers may take a computing cluster years to crack. Therefore, most successful cyberattacks on encrypted data these days don't crack the cipher itself, but rather the implementation of the cipher. Think of it this way: I could have a thick iron door with tight hinges and a rock-solid physical lock. But if I leave the key in a place where a burglar can find it, the strength of my door and its lock become pointless. Unfortunately, cyberattackers can often find the decryption keys to the strongest ciphers out there. For instance, sometimes decryption keys are mistakenly put in areas of the

Internet that are publicly accessible. Improper encryption implementation is one of the most frequent problems occurring in the information security facet of confidentiality.

Integrity is making sure that data isn't changed, altered, or removed without authorization. If a cyberattacker penetrates my home PC and deletes folders and files off my hard drive, that's an attack on the integrity of my data. *Malware* infection can be a threat to integrity, too. (Malware is all harmful software. We'll explain that very soon in this chapter.) Those malicious executables aren't supposed to be on my computer! Cryptographic hash functions are often used to check the integrity of data. An example is when files can be downloaded on the Internet, and MD5 and SHA2 hashes for these files are provided for users. If the data in the files is tampered with in any way, the hash function can be checked. If hashing the file returns a different result, don't touch that file! Someone has messed around with it.

Availability means that data is there when it's needed. One of the most common cyberattacks on availability is *distributed denial of service (DDoS) attacks*. These attacks occur when a distributed group of computers sends a target, such as a point on a network, way more packets of data than it's designed to handle. The memory buffers in computer systems overflow with excess data, and then the affected computers become unavailable. Web servers are frequent targets of DDoS attacks.

DDoS attacks are relatively minor as far as cyberattacks are concerned. A typical enterprise network is hit with dozens of DDoS attempts per week, and a network can recover from a DDoS attack simply by rebooting the servers and client computers that are affected. Nevertheless, there are two major reasons why security practitioners should prevent DDoS attacks.

The first reason is that computer service providers try to make sure that their systems have as much uptime as possible. Computers that go out of service means that employees, customers, or clientele have to go without their necessary computer services for a given period of time. GitHub (github.com) has a massive collection of software repositories that hundreds of thousands of software developers use every day. If enough GitHub servers were DDoS attacked to make the service slow, unreliable, or completely unavailable, there would be a lot of very unhappy computer programmers! Or, if Facebook was significantly affected by DDoS attacks, a lot of its users around the world would be very upset.

The second reason why DDoS attacks should be prevented is that they're often the first step an advanced persistent threat (APT) or cyberattacker group takes in order to conduct much more destructive cyberattacks. Network administrators can be distracted by the effects of a DDoS attack, so an APT group can conduct another means of network penetration without being noticed. Or, if firewalls and intrusion prevention systems get DDoS attacked, a much worse cyberattack may go unnoticed by an enterprise's security information and event management (SIEM) system. There are many other cyberattacks on the availability of data, but as a pentester you may be simulating DDoS attacks quite often!

As I mentioned, some cyberattacks can affect more than one component of the CIA triad. For example, if a cyberattacker puts a remote access Trojan (RAT) on a targeted machine, the confidentiality of data is threatened because a cybercriminal can see files that they're not authorized to access. The criminal could delete files and folders on the computer's hard drives, which affects the integrity of data. Then the attacker could delete the firmware on the router that the computer uses to access the Internet (that's *integrity* again), making it impossible for the computer's rightful owner to access their data remotely. That's an attack on the availability of their data.

Security Controls

Security controls are the means and ways of protecting the information security of computer systems. Enforcing and implementing them is a blue team matter, but penetration testing them is a red team matter. When you pentest, you'll be testing the effectiveness of the security controls in your targeted system. Here's a brief summary of them.

ISO/IEC 27002 (www.iso.org/standard/54533.html) is a standard from the International Organization for Standardization and the International Electrotechnical Commission that defines security controls. The document is called *Information technology – Security techniques – Code of practice for information security controls*. The following explanations of different categories of security controls are based on it.

Administrative controls are the policies, guidelines, standards, and procedures that an organization designs to manage how activities can be conducted in a secure way. These controls also include regulations and laws enacted by government bodies. For instance, the General Data Protection Regulation (GDPR) (gdpr-info.eu) in the European Union regulates how data pertaining to European individuals and entities should be managed securely. When a data breach affects European data, the GDPR regulates how such incidents should be reported and what the penalties are for any parties considered to be guilty for their part in the incident. More importantly, the GDPR regulates how data should be securely stored and transmitted.

It's common for organizations to have information security policies. Those are some of the most fundamental administrative controls in security. Does the company have a Bring Your Own Device policy, and if so, how should employees be using their devices and connecting them to the corporate networks? Who in the organization gets administrative access to the company's networks, and which user rights should other specific employees and their user groups have? These are all examples of administrative controls. People often forget that information security isn't only a technical area of study, it's also a human area of study—what people are allowed to do with computer systems and how they do it is crucial to information security as a whole.

Logical controls are what most people consider first when thinking about security controls. These controls are things like firewalls, passwords, intrusion detection systems, access control lists, encryption, antivirus software, biometric authentication systems, second-factor authentication codes, CAPTCHAs, and other facets of secure software design and the software that manages security in some direct way or another.

The principle of *least privilege* is a very common and important logical control. It means that people should only have access to the data and computer systems they need to do their work—and absolutely no more. A payroll clerk needs access to payroll systems and their own email. A payroll clerk doesn't need access to anyone else's email or to the Active Directory implementation that the network administrator uses to control who has access to what on Windows machines. By making sure that employees and other users can't access data and computer systems that they don't need, access to sensitive data and computers is limited, making the network more secure.

Physical controls ensure that people don't have unauthorized physical access to computer systems and data. Locks on doors to the server room make sure that the only people who can touch an enterprise's servers with their own hands are those who need to have access to them to keep their network's backend going. Closed-circuit television cameras that are properly positioned will enable security guards to see that no one walks into the office who doesn't work there. Walls, fences, receptionists, smoke alarms, HVAC systems, and barricades are other examples of physical controls. Keeping the on-premises network and workplace correctly physically segmented is another type of physical control. As a pentester, you might have to test physical security by crawling through duct work or trying to pick physical locks! Pentesting physical controls can be a lot of fun. Imitate scenes from *Die Hard* and pretend you're Bruce Willis. You chose the right career for adventure, ethical hacker!

Access Control

Access control is often considered to be the bedrock of most information security measures. Keeping information secure is about making sure that only authorized parties have access to the specific components of information systems. Access control usually pertains to the confidentiality part of the CIA triad. But it can also pertain to integrity; that is, making sure that only authorized parties can alter particular data. Sometimes, access control applies to availability, too. An information system may only have the capability for its authorized parties to access it. If a bunch of unauthorized parties acquire access, it can make the information unavailable.

Access control applies to software, hardware, networking, and physical security alike. The lock on your front door ensures that only you have physical access to your home. The same concept applies to your user account on your home PC's operating system. If you alone have your password, then only you have digital access to your computer's operating system.

Therefore, access control is a function that applies to the majority of the different types of security controls that are defined in the ISO/IEC 27002 standard.

For a home PC, you can implement a simple access control scheme. Access control gets a lot more complex when it needs to apply to enterprises with physical office buildings, hundreds of client machines, server rooms, on-premises and cloud networks, and so on. In these more complex applications, information security theory defines access control practices that can scale very well according to the particular needs of an information system. Following are some of the most commonly implemented access control practices.

Role-based Access Control

Role-based access control (RBAC) permits access according to a user's role within an organization. It's the practice that you'll see most often in network settings. That's because it's a very efficient way to implement the principle of least privilege. Accountants can be put into an accounting group and be given access to the financial servers. However, they will not be given access to the machines that network administrators use to manage the network.

The network administrators can be put into a group that gives them "admin" access to Active Directory, or whichever application is being used to manage the access control lists. In this case, however, they can deny themselves write permissions to the financial servers, and so forth. Because specific permissions can be granted to user groups, and users are put into user groups according to their roles, a lot of time and energy is saved when compared to designating permissions for each individual user.

Mandatory Access Control

Mandatory access control (MAC) is often used in environments with very strict security needs. It's associated with the multilevel security systems that were designed to protect data that has been classified by military and intelligence agencies. But MAC has evolved to be used well beyond military and intelligence networks. For instance, you will often see MAC in the financial services industry as well.

In a MAC system, security policy is typically centrally controlled by a security policy administrator. Users cannot delegate permissions themselves. For instance, the creator of a text file cannot decide its read/write permissions. Unlike in a RBAC environment, however, permissions in a MAC system are usually assigned to objects like operating system processes, I/O devices, files and folders, and so on, as opposed to human users. In a MAC system, security policy is constrained according to system classification, configuration, and authentication.

Discretionary Access Control

Discretionary access control (DAC) is the third major access control practice you'll often see as a pentester. The United States Department of Defense's Trusted Computer System Evaluation Criteria (TCSEC) define DAC as "a means of restricting access to objects based on the identity of subjects and/or groups to which they belong. The controls are discretionary in the sense that a subject with a certain access permission is capable of passing that permission (perhaps indirectly) on to any other subject (unless restrained by mandatory access control)." Therefore, DAC can be blended with RBAC and MAC schemes in order to comply with specific information security standards and regulations.

The example cited of the creator of a text file delegating its read/write permissions is a typical DAC method. But because TCSEC doesn't define implementation specifics, you'll see DAC used in many different ways.

Incident Response

Incident response is how organizations respond to cyberattacks. If the simulated cyberattacks you conduct in your pentesting were real cyberattacks by real cyberattackers, specific policies and procedures would define how an organization must react.

Effective incident response can make all the difference when it comes to the impact of a cyberattack. Ideally, an organization will have a designated incident response team and written incident response policies, and it will learn from the cyberattacks to which they respond in order to securely harden their networks further. Just as organizations should learn from your pentests how to mitigate the vulnerabilities that you discover, they should also apply lessons learned from actual cyberattacks. Incident response teams are often called CSIRTs, short for computer security incident response teams. They usually consist of security and general IT staff, along with members of the legal, human resources, and public relations departments.

The National Institute of Standards and Technology (NIST) has a Computer Security Incident Handling Guide, NIST Special Publication 800-61 (csrc .nist.gov/publications/detail/sp/800-61/archive/2004-01-16) that defines the various stages of effective incident response.

Preparation

The first step is *preparation*. It may not be the CSIRT's responsibility to prevent cyberattacks, but they must be prepared to respond to them. So, the first step should be in place before any incidents occur.

Know who to contact when an incident is detected. Every member of a CSIRT team should have that information. CSIRT members and any parties that must be contacted when an incident is discovered should be able to communicate with each other and act quickly. Network administrators in the CSIRT should make sure that any devices on their networks that can be logged have logs. They should also make sure that intrusion detection systems, firewalls, anti-malware, and security information and event management systems (SIEM) are working and in place, however they may be applicable. These actions will ensure that if an incident indeed occurs, it can be detected and responded to quickly.

Moving on, make sure that there's documentation for all of the hardware, software, network devices, and cloud platforms that the organization uses. The CSIRT should also make sure that people in the organization know how to report incidents and that some people in their incident response team have administrative access to your various systems. Do these things while still being mindful of the principle of least privilege, of course. And the CSIRT should make sure that everyone involved has specific security training, with periodic refreshers and reminders.

Detection and Analysis

The next step is *detection and analysis*. The detection systems from the previous step will identify an anomaly in network behavior, a data breach, malware, or some other indication of compromise. The anomaly should be investigated as to whether or not it's a false positive. If it's a true positive, further analysis should be done to understand its nature, implications, and source. Where did the incident come from?

There are various ways and means of detecting and analyzing cyber incidents, including but not limited to human beings observing suspicious activity, SIEM alerts, alerts from other types of security solutions, anti-malware, file integrity checking software, data loss prevention systems, and logs pertaining to user behavior, applications, cloud services, external storage, memory, network devices, and operating systems.

Containment, Eradication, and Recovery

The third step is *containment, eradication, and recovery*. Once the metaphorical fire has been found, it's time to make sure that it is extinguished so that it doesn't spread!

Many types of incidents, such as malware and data breaches, can be contained. Containment strategies will be different for each type of cyberattack. In the containment process, network administrators may have to shut down or disconnect network segments or particular computers, disable certain functions or user accounts, or redirect a cyberattack to a sandbox or honeypot. A *sandbox* is an environment that can run software without affecting the rest of the operating system, whereas a *honeypot* is a computer that's actually designed to attract cyberattacks so that other parts of the network don't get attacked. Think of honeypots like lightning rods on tall buildings.

Evidence needs to be gathered that can be used to investigate an incident in the following step. Who handled the evidence? Which logs pertain to the incident? What's the pertinent identification information, such as IP addresses, MAC addresses, user accounts, serial numbers, or hostnames?

The sources of the incident may need to be eradicated, such as particular applications, user accounts, or malicious files.

Then they must recover from the incident, restoring systems to normal operation, restoring data from backups, and changing passwords or other means of authentication. Other recovery actions include installing patches and reconfiguring firewalls. You must do everything that applies to the particular nature of the incident.

Post-incident Activity

The final step is *post-incident activity*. The organization may hire an outside security firm to help investigate what happened and how similar incidents can be prevented in the future. Either way, members of the CSIRT must have a "lessons learned" meeting to prevent similar incidents from happening in the future, and also perhaps to improve incident response procedures—what happened and when? How did the incident happen? What were the vulnerabilities and exploits that were involved? How can your computers and networks be better security hardened? Do any policies or procedures need to be improved? Does your staff need more security training?

Sometimes as a red teamer, you may be pentesting in synchronicity with an organization's incident response policies. So, although CSIRTs are a blue team matter, you will often need to collaborate with the blue team.

Malware

Malware is all malicious software. People often refer to any kind of malware as a virus, but computer viruses are just one of the many types of malware.

What is and isn't malware can sometimes be subjective. In the past, some popular applications were considered to be spyware because they track user activity through the developers' servers, without the knowledge of the user. Is that a cyberattack on the confidentiality of an individual's data? Some people would say yes, because the user didn't explicitly consent to being monitored. But the developer may claim that the user consented to being monitored by installing the application in the first place.

As a pentester, you might use malware in your work. Your client has to determine what is and isn't permitted when you use malware to simulate cyberattacks, and you must abide by that. Also, you must not execute malware on any computer without the owner's permission. This includes making sure that the malware isn't transmitted through the public Internet where it could possibly infect millions of machines. For that reason, you may need to test malware within virtual machines only in order to sandbox the malware properly from doing any harm to actual computers. A virtual machine can be configured from disc images to replicate the operating systems, applications, and configurations perfectly that are used on the real computers deployed in the network on which you're performing penetration testing. In most countries around the world, developing, possessing, and deploying malware in and of itself is legal, with the very important condition that it's *used only with the explicit consent of the owners of the computers and networks on which it's being tested*. Without that consent, deploying malware is illegal and can result in criminal punishment!

Malware can be categorized according to its behavior and how it replicates from one computer to another.

Viruses

Viruses replicate by infecting a file, or multiple files, on a computer and then they copy themselves onto other computers through networks (such as the Internet or a company's LAN) or through removable media such as CDs, DVDs, and USB drives. These days, the Internet is the most common way that viruses spread. Because viruses were the most common type of malware in the early days of personal computing, people learned to call all malware viruses. However, viruses are only one kind of malware.

Worms

Worms are another way to classify malware according to how it spreads from computer to computer. Unlike viruses, worms carry themselves in their own containers rather than needing to alter the contents of existing files on their target. Like viruses, however, worms date back to the good old days and are still a common type of malware today. They can also spread through networks and removable media.

Fileless Malware

Fileless malware is a relatively recent phenomenon, but it is a quickly growing problem on all kinds of computers and operating systems. Technically speaking, it does have files, like any data. However, it doesn't write any files on a target's data storage, such as a hard drive. Fileless malware operates completely from the memory of its target machine. Therefore, there isn't a file on a hard drive that can be detected in an antivirus scan. Antivirus evasion is why fileless malware is becoming really popular with cyberattackers. They can cyberattack much more effectively while undetected!

The most common way that fileless malware works is by infecting an operating system process on its target machine. In Windows, processes can be seen by opening Task Manager or Process Explorer. Other operating system platforms have different applications that can be used to see which processes are running. Because of the covert nature of fileless malware, it's usually detected by observing the behavior of an infected machine.

Ransomware

Ransomware describes how this type of malware behaves. Ransomware works by encrypting the files on its target's data storage with a decryption key that's inaccessible to the victim. Ransomware is designed to show a ransom note to the victim, which is often done through a text file or a local web page. The ransom note typically explains that the victim's files were encrypted, and that they'll need to pay the attacker money—the ransom—in order to get their files back.

In the early 2000s, ransoms were usually paid by making the victim enter their credit card number. These days, attackers will usually demand that their victims pay their ransoms with cryptocurrency.

The first major cryptocurrency, Bitcoin, debuted in 2009. For all of the benefits of cryptocurrency, it also provided cyberattackers with a way to profit from their cyberattacks that was a lot more difficult for investigators to trace. That's why you'll rarely see ransomware demand credit card numbers nowadays. Ransomware is considered to be an attack on the availability of data.

Cryptominers

Cryptominers aren't always malware. They use computer processing power to solve complex mathematical problems in order to generate cryptocurrency. Sometimes, a user will consent to allowing a cryptominer to operate on their machine. A cryptominer could be generating cryptocurrency for the user on machines that the user owns, or a user could consent to cryptomining for a developer in order to enjoy a website or application free of charge. When cryptominers run with the user's consent, they aren't malware.

Nonetheless, cyberattackers will often execute cryptominers without the consent of the owners of the machines on which they're running them. That's when cryptominers are malware. Attackers may have a botnet with thousands or millions of victim (zombie) machines so that the computer processing power used on any individual machine is minimal enough to evade detection.

Botnets

Botnets are networks of machines that are infected with zombie malware that allows a cyberattacker to control them. Cyberattackers use command and control servers to synchronize all of the zombies in their botnet to execute large-scale attacks. Botnets are also often used to execute DDoS attacks.

Spyware

Spyware is malware that threatens a victim's confidentiality. As the name suggests, spyware spies on users. It shows cyberattackers some or all of the activities or data on infected computers. For example, spyware might send an attacker data about your web activity or email.

Trojans

Trojans are named after the Trojan horse of Greek mythology. A *Trojan* is a file or application that appears to the user as something that they want, but in reality, malware is embedded in the Trojan. For example, a ransomware file that's bound to a photo attached to an email is a Trojan. Some of the popular free screensavers in the 1990s were Trojans. Trojans can take many forms, but they require user cooperation in order to be executed, so they must disguise themselves as something that the victim wants.

Rootkits

Rootkits acquire unauthorized access to targeted machines, and they try very hard to evade detection. Root is a word that's often used to mean administrative access to a computer, hence its name. A rootkit's malicious actions are those that would require administrative access. For example, let's say that your home PC runs Kubuntu, a version of Linux. In Linux or UNIX-based systems, users need to enter an administrative password every time they want to do something that requires "root" access, such as when you install new applications from a repository. Rootkits can be very dangerous indeed, because they can possibly do anything to a computer's operating system and applications that you can imagine!

Modular Malware

Modular malware is a relatively new cyber threat. Modular malware doesn't just do one thing or another. Rather, it consists of multiple modules that can each perform different kinds of malicious behavior. Modular malware initially appeared on Android devices. Now there's lots of modular malware for pretty much every popular operating system platform on mobile, desktops, and servers alike.

Here's how modular malware usually works. The first component infects a target machine to establish a connection and access for a cyberattacker's *command and control servers*. Then, over a period of time, the attacker's command and control servers upload a number of different modules. One module could be a rootkit. The next module could be spyware. The following module could be a cryptominer. Cyberattackers that use modular malware try multiple ways to profit financially from their victims, and it's often deployed by advanced persistent threat groups.

So, malware can belong to multiple categories. Spyware can be a worm if that's how it replicates. A rootkit can be a virus. A malicious cryptominer can be fileless malware. Malware was a problem with computers years before personal computers emerged in the late 1970s. And malware is now a bigger problem than ever as the cyber threat landscape continuously evolves.

Advanced Persistent Threats

Advanced persistent threats (APTs) consist of targeted cyberattacks that stay on victims' computers for a long time, possibly months or years, while undetected. They usually come from sophisticated nation-state sponsored cyberattack groups as a part of military cyberwarfare programs. Some APTs nowadays also come from organized crime groups.

Kinetic warfare is still with us, as it has been for thousands of years. But as the years go on, more and more military activity is done on computers through the Internet. Sometimes APT groups target utilities like power plants or factories. They often have SCADA systems that are connected to the public Internet, so a lot of damage can be done. At other times, APTs can target office networks, looking for sensitive information or to make a lot of money by infecting many computers with ransomware or malicious cryptominers. It's also not unheard of for APTs to target consumers and their ordinary PC and smartphone endpoints.

APTs are also used in red team operations to simulate real-world cyberattacks. MITRE ATT&CK (Adversarial Tactics, Techniques & Common Knowledge) Framework (`attack.mitre.org`) is a globally accessible knowledge base of adversary tactics and techniques based on real-world observations. The APTs from MITRE ATT&CK detail the latest tactics, techniques, and procedures (TTPs), which can be used to emulate cyberattacks.

The Cyber Kill Chain

Now that you understand what APTs are all about, we'll summarize a methodology for how to deal with them. As a pentester, you won't be responding to real cyberattacks, but it helps to understand what the blue team and security operations center do so that you can appreciate how the vulnerability information you give them may be applied. A holistic understanding of cybersecurity will help you to become a more effective ethical hacker!

The kill chain concept originates with kinetic warfare. It involves identifying a target, dispatching the appropriate troops, figuring out how to attack the target effectively according to the context and conditions of battle, and destroying the target.

Here's an example of a kill chain methodology that's been commonly used in kinetic warfare for decades.

F2T2EA is an acronym for its phases:

Find: Identify a target through intelligence, surveillance, or reconnaissance.

Fix: Acquire coordinates for the target.

Track: Monitor the target's movement.

Target: Choose the appropriate weapon, assess the value of the target, and check the availability of weapons or other means of attack.

Engage: Strike the target!

Assess: Evaluate how the attack went and gather intelligence.

Military contractor Lockheed-Martin developed a kill chain for cybersecurity purposes. The *Cyber Kill Chain* was published in 2011, designed by computer scientists to address APTs through computer networks. You can read this document for more information.

```
www.lockheedmartin.com/content/dam/lockheed-martin/rms/documents/
cyber/Gaining_the_Advantage_Cyber_Kill_Chain.pdf
```

The Cyber Kill Chain consists of the following phases and actions that APTs often take in their attacks:

Reconnaissance: The cyberattacker or adversary researches their target, looking for vulnerabilities. They could be harvesting email addresses, seeking out employees on social media (especially LinkedIn), looking for Internet-facing servers, and so on.

Weaponization: The attacker develops or procures malware for remote access that exploits vulnerabilities found in the reconnaissance phase.

Delivery: Malware is delivered to the target through USB drives, email, phishing sites, compromised websites known as "watering holes," social media, and so on.

Exploitation: The malware starts its work. It could be triggered by a human victim interacting with a Trojan, command and control servers, or some other means.

Installation: Malware is installed by the actions in the previous phase. A shell could be installed for remote command execution, a backdoor could be created, or the cyberattacker could acquire a control interface in some other way.

Command and Control: The attacker uses the control interface established in the previous phase. A two-way communication channel is created in a covert fashion.

Actions on Objectives: Now the APT gets what it wants from its target. This phase could involve data theft and corruption, privilege escalation, credential acquisition, or other such malicious actions.

Common Vulnerabilities and Exposures

As a pentester, your job is to discover vulnerabilities. Vulnerabilities fall into two basic categories: zero-day vulnerabilities, which are unknown to cyber-attack targets until a malicious actor exploits them, and vulnerabilities in hardware, software, and networking devices that you already know about.

In your work, you'll be surprised by how many known vulnerabilities get exploited by cyberattackers. If a vulnerability is already public knowledge, why wouldn't an organization mitigate it? Sometimes, for pragmatic reasons, organizations need to use legacy technology for compatibility. At other times organizations have trouble convincing their C-suite executives to invest in technology upgrades. And sometimes people are just sloppy.

Known vulnerabilities are usually, but not always, recorded in the *Common Vulnerabilities and Exposures (CVE) system*. If someone specializes in pentesting or red teaming, they may ask you, "Do you have any CVEs?" meaning whether you have made any contributions to the ever-growing CVE database. If you go on to having a successful pentesting or bug hunting career from reading this book, you may have CVEs of your own someday.

The CVE database is available to anyone with access to the web. Take a look at it yourself at cve.mitre.org.

Each recorded vulnerability in the CVE database is numbered using this format:

CVE-(four digit year)-(four digit number unique to the year)

The year is when the vulnerability was discovered, of course. For illustrative purposes, we chose a random CVE from 2020, CVE-2020-7060.

This is the standard format for recording vulnerabilities in the CVE:

CVE-ID: CVE-2020-7060

Description: "When using certain `mbstring` functions to convert multibyte encodings, in PHP versions 7.2.x below 7.2.27, 7.3.x below 7.3.14, and 7.4.x below 7.4.2, it is possible to supply data that will cause function `mbfl_filt_conv_big5_wchar` to read past the allocated buffer. This may lead to information disclosure or crash."

References: A group of URLs with information about this specific vulnerability.

Assigning CNA: PHP Group. (CNA = CVE Numbering Authority, an organization that contributes to the CVE.)

Date Entry Created: `20200115` (The format is year, month, day.) A disclaimer says, "The entry creation date may reflect when the CVE ID was allocated or reserved, and does not necessarily indicate when this vulnerability was discovered, shared with the affected vendor, publicly disclosed, or updated in CVE."

There are four legacy sections that are basically empty: phase, votes, comments, and proposed. You may see these sections filled in on older reported vulnerabilities.

Feel free to browse the CVE database yourself when you have the time. As a pentester, this is a glimpse into your world now!

Phishing and Other Social Engineering

As a pentester, you may imitate cyberattackers by simulating social engineering attacks. *Social engineering* is any malicious action that involves fooling human beings. In a sense, social engineering has existed long before the advent of modern computing. Scams, tricks, and manipulative dishonesty has existed for pretty much the entirety of human history; only now, people are fooled through the technological wonder of computers.

Kevin Mitnick is one of the most famous (or infamous) malicious hackers ever. Many people might not know this, but the cyberattacks Mitnick conducted in the 1970s and 1980s were mainly done through social engineering. When he was twelve, Mitnick fooled a bus driver into helping him acquire a ticket puncher for the Los Angeles bus system's punch cards in order to ride for free. He lied by telling the bus driver that the ticket punch was for a school project. He refined his intel gathering methods to acquire passwords, usernames, and modem phone numbers in later social engineering attacks. All he did was lie to his targets. As a pentester, you might phone or email receptionists, call center agents, or other human targets to see if you can acquire information that they're not supposed to give you.

There's one means of social engineering that really needed computer technology to exist, and that's phishing. *Phishing* is when a website, text message, or email is designed to spoof a legitimate entity that your target trusts. The spoofed entity could be a bank, an online service like Netflix or Amazon, a utility company, a government agency, or any organization with which the target is familiar and whom the target trusts.

A common type of phishing attack involves creating a phishing website that imitates a website belonging to a trusted entity and then enticing the user to enter their username and password into a web form on the entity that's being spoofed. Another common type of phishing attack involves sending the target an email or text message that spoofs the trusted entity, luring them to click a link that opens a web page which transmits malware to the target's machine.

Spear phishing is when a phishing attack has a very specific target that the attacker has researched, which is a type of cyberattack that APTs often conduct. Other kinds of phishing may be less targeted, as it is basically sent to random victims to see who succumbs.

Phishing attacks are now easier to conduct than ever before. Cyberattackers can buy phishing kits from dark web markets that have all of the files they need to create a phishing website or email that spoofs what a particular trusted entity uses.

Airgapped Machines

As a pentester, you may occasionally encounter an airgapped machine. If and when you do, you're up for a real challenge!

An *airgapped machine* is isolated from as many cyberattack vectors as possible. It won't be connected to any unsecured networks, especially not the public Internet. A really seriously airgapped machine may not be connected to any networks at all. Cyberattacks can sometimes be conducted through removable media or USB devices, so optical drives may be removed or disabled. USB ports are usually disabled. If you need a way to get new data onto an airgapped computer other than through mouse and keyboard input, there may be a removable media interface behind a lock or means of authentication to which only one or a few users have access. And, of course, an airgapped computer is usually in a room with physical and electronic locks that only permit a few specially designated users physical access.

Airgapped machines are normally used to secure highly classified data. Obviously, an airgapped computer is really inconvenient to use, so they're used only when absolutely necessary.

So how could an airgapped machine possibly be cyberattacked? You'd be surprised! Researchers once found a method to penetrate airgapped machines in use by placing a camera that could see the machine through a server room window and record how the hard drive light blinked. The light-blinking patterns could then be used to determine the data that was being written. Mind-blowing, eh? Another means of attacking an airgapped machine would be to bribe one of the few individuals who have physical access to it into carrying out a cyberattack. Humans are often the weakest link!

The Dark Web

The *dark web* sounds ominous. Once you understand it a bit, however, it won't seem so exotic or scary. As a pentester, you should understand the role that the dark web plays in cyberattacks.

There are encrypted networks that route the Internet through proxy servers. Two of the most commonly used encrypted proxy networks are Tor and I2P.

Tor stands for The Onion Router, and it was first deployed in 2002. *I2P* stands for the Invisible Internet Project, and it was first deployed in 2003. The existence of these networks and their use, in and of itself, is legal as long as you're not in China. (The Chinese government uses laws and technologies to restrict citizens' access to the Internet significantly in a system that's often called the Great Firewall of China. Many Chinese do break out of the Great Firewall of China, but doing so is illegal.) In fact, the networks were developed with military technology by both public- and private-sector computer scientists. The Internet outside these encrypted proxy networks is often called the "clearnet." That's the public Internet that you typically use. On the clearnet, your Internet traffic can usually be traced through your gateway IP address and the paths that data takes to and from your endpoint from server to server.

On Tor and I2P, a new IP address is used for each proxy node so that the end-points and servers can usually only be traced to the nearest node.

All that you need to use Tor or I2P is a special application on your PC or mobile device. For example, if you want to use the web through Tor, you can install the Tor Browser. It's possible to route most of your usual Internet use through these proxy networks. However, there are also websites that you can only access through Tor or I2P, and those websites are what the dark web is all about. Tor-exclusive websites use the .onion top-level domain, and I2P-exclusive use the .i2p top-level domain.

Not all dark web use is illicit. Sometimes, investigative journalists and political activists in hostile areas of the world use the dark web to communicate messages that are in the public interest, safely and without government interference. In most of the world outside of China, simply using the dark web is legal. Generally, only if you use the dark web to violate the criminal code of your jurisdiction is it illegal.

The dark web has many websites that use a model based on eBay to sell illegal goods and services. Those are what we refer to as *dark web markets*. If buyers and sellers with anonymizing usernames have a reputation for honest behavior, they will have positive ratings from the dark web market community. This works much in the same way as buyer and seller reputations on eBay, except that the dark web is geared toward selling illegal and illicit things. Those things can include illegal drugs and firearms. What's relevant to the field of information security is that dark web markets are also used to sell malware, exploit kits, databases of credit card information and other sensitive data, and phishing kits.

Dark web markets only accept cryptocurrency as payment, as cryptocurrency transactions are more difficult to trace than credit card or PayPal transactions.

The advent of dark web markets has facilitated cybercrime worldwide. You don't need to be a good programmer or computer scientist to conduct sophisticated cyberattacks. For enough Bitcoin, you can buy malware, exploits, breached information, and the files you need to create phishing websites and emails.

Summary

You must start your journey to becoming a pentester by understanding the basics of computers and cybersecurity.

Computers run operating systems, which is software within which all of your applications run. PCs, mobile devices, and servers are all different types of computers, and they all have their own operating system platforms.

Computers can communicate with other computers through networks. Networks are wired and wireless communication means for computer data. The Internet is a type of network, but there are smaller private networks that operate in commercial and industrial workplaces and consumer households alike.

CompTIA offers certifications that are useful to establish a general understanding of information technology, such as the A+, Network+, and Security+ certifications. Pentesters can use those certifications to demonstrate that they have a good general understanding of information technology.

Information security, computer security, cybersecurity, and network security are overlapping terms. But they can all apply to the security of computer data.

Information security theory is based on concepts like the CIA triad, access control, and the principle of least privilege.

There are various areas of information security that you should understand in order to be an effective pentester. They include malware, APTs, the Cyber Kill Chain, social engineering, the dark web, and different types of security controls. Incident response and CSIRTs are a blue team area, unlike pentesting, which is a red team area. As a pentester, however, you should understand what the blue team does to appreciate how the vulnerabilities that you discover will benefit them in their security hardening. Blue teams and red teams often need to collaborate.

3

Education of a Hacker

Many would-be pentesters come from system admin, network security, and application security backgrounds, and though they have some experience with vulnerability scanners, their hacking knowledge may be lacking. Learning to hack can be challenging, and this is often the most difficult part of becoming a pentester. So, starting out, future pentesters have to focus their energy on learning how to hack.

In this chapter we will cover hacking skills, the hacker mindset, and the Pentester Blueprint Formula for becoming a pentester.

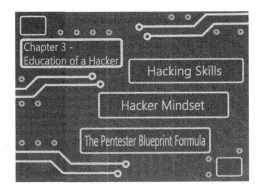

Hacking Skills

Learning to hack is an important part of pentesting, and it is required to go beyond performing security vulnerability assessments. Hacking is the part of pentesting that makes it so attractive to those wanting to become pentesters. Hacking skills are best developed through hands-on experience and repetition, and as you develop your knowledge and hacking skills, you will build your base knowledge of vulnerabilities and how to exploit them. This will help you to reduce the research time required for the easier exploits and improve your efficiency.

It's important to keep notes on how to validate and exploit vulnerabilities. Note-taking applications like OneNote, Evernote, Keepnote, and Cherry Tree make note taking and organization easier and more effective. Evernote has a web clipping function that allows you to clip sections of articles from websites and blogs. You can save the whole page or a just a section.

You can learn hacking and pentesting in several ways. Just as with other subjects, books, websites, blogs, and courses are available. Some colleges offer pentesting courses, which are often referred to as ethical hacking courses. Conferences offer learning opportunities through talks, workshops, and pre-conference training. Information security groups have presentations on hacking and other security subjects. Some companies offer pentesting and ethical hacking courses, such as the SANS Institute and Cybary. Several offer online courses, making it less expensive since travel is not required. These online options are self-paced, allowing you to learn at your own pace and on your own schedule.

Hacker Mindset

An important part of becoming a pentester is developing the *hacker mindset*, which is the ability to think like a hacker and be able to find ways to exploit vulnerabilities. The hacker mindset is a culmination of creative and analytical thinking. Developing this mindset is like learning how to troubleshoot. Installing software or hardware can be easy and straightforward, but when you run into problems and must work through those problems, you learn how to troubleshoot.

When you find a vulnerability and try to exploit it, the exploit might not work. Not all exploits work all of the time, and you must work through the options or try other exploits. You learn to put together different exploits to help you reach the goal of the information you are trying to access. This might require admin or root level access to accomplish, or you may function just as a regular user would, but you must work through the vulnerability until you have exhausted all possibilities. Not all vulnerabilities are exploitable, but you need to ensure that they can't be exploited.

The hacker mindset takes time and repetition to develop, and it is best developed by hands-on hacking experience.

The Pentester Blueprint Formula

To become a pentester, you must understand the technologies and security of the targets that you are hacking, and you must have the hacker mindset. These three elements make up the Pentester Blueprint. A common mistake of many aspiring pentesters is to underestimate the importance of technology. Working as a system admin and having infosec background, for example, can provide valuable experience that will help you become a pentester. As another example, people with experience in web application development will pick up web application pentesting easier than those without that experience (see Figure 3.1).

Figure 3.1: The Pentester Blueprint Formula

In Chapter 2, we covered the prerequisite knowledge needed before learning how to hack. In Chapter 4, we will discuss resources that can help you acquire the hacking knowledge and skills required to become a pentester.

Ethical Hacking Areas

Pentesting and ethical hacking entail many different areas. You could be hacking applications, hardware, networks, or even human beings! Hacking human beings is often referred to as *social engineering*. Have you ever received a phone call saying that the IRS will arrest you if you don't send Bitcoin to the caller? Have you ever seen a web page saying that you were the site's one millionth visitor, and you should input your personal banking information to be awarded a monetary prize? Congratulations, you've witnessed social engineering attacks.

Some pentesters do a variety of types of ethical hacking, some specializing in one area or another. Following is a summary of the various areas of penetration testing.

Operating Systems and Applications

Pentesters can test particular installations of operating systems and the applications running within them. A wide range of software vulnerabilities are known and recorded in vulnerability collections, such as the *Common Vulnerabilities and Exposures (CVE)* database. Sometimes, ethical hackers who target software can even find *zero-day vulnerabilities*, which are vulnerabilities that were previously unknown. People who participate in bug bounty programs are often on the hunt for zero-day vulnerabilities, and they're rewarded handsomely with large sums of money.

Vulnerabilities are found in code all of the time. Ask any computer programmer—it's often impossible to program anything without some bugs! And sometimes bugs are actual security problems that can be exploited.

Software applications aren't the only programs that run directly on a computer. Web applications are also a common target of cyberattackers and ethical hackers alike. We check our email, perhaps send out tweets, and visit many websites every day. Web development code is a lot more sophisticated than it was in the late 1990s; full-fledged web applications now run in your web browser, and are a growing target of cyberattackers, so pentesters need to test those applications as well.

Networks

Networks are another target for pentesters. They are composed of devices such as routers, firewalls, and switches. They may test networks that are on an organization's premises, on a cloud service like Amazon Web Services (AWS), or a hybrid network (a combination of a network on a company's premises and a network on a third-party cloud service). Networks can be implemented and configured in many different ways, and ethical hackers test all of them.

The following is a concise explanation of the different types of networks.

Local Area Network

A *local area network (LAN)* is a small network that usually has fewer than 50 endpoints, and they exist in the same physical area, such as a small office or in a person's home. An *endpoint* is a computer that's used to interact with a network. LANs are often found at home, so typical endpoints these days can be PCs, video game consoles, smartphones, and Internet of Things (IoT) devices, such as Amazon Echo or Google Home smart speakers. If a LAN is deployed through Wi-Fi, it can also be called a WLAN or wireless LAN.

Personal Area Network

You will rarely see the term *personal area network (PAN)*. A PAN is a LAN that's inside your home. So, in that context, PANs and LANs are the same thing.

Wide Area Network

Wide area networks (WAN) exist when businesses and institutions connect more than one of their own LANs together. A LAN exists in one location, such as in an office. A WAN occupies multiple physical locations. So, for example, a WAN could be a company's office LAN in Toronto connected to the company's other LANs in the Dallas and Chicago offices. Because nearly everyone has a LAN at home these days, some people consider the Internet to be a massive WAN!

Metropolitan Area Network

A *metropolitan area network (MAN)* is a term that you'll see less often. The one major difference between a WAN and a MAN is that the latter has to serve a geographical area between 5 and 50 kilometers in range. If the network exists in a larger range than 50 kilometers, such as the Toronto, Dallas, Chicago example given previously, that's a WAN, not a MAN.

As we mentioned, pentesters may be called upon to test on premises, in the cloud, or on hybrid cloud networks. In the 1990s, a corporate network would typically be on a company's own premises, perhaps as a WAN or MAN, linking multiple offices. In the 21st century, companies like Amazon, Google, and Oracle started to provide their own cloud computing platforms for other businesses. That opened up an opportunity for a company's network to be entirely based on a cloud platform, or to combine the cloud with its on-premises network in what we call a *hybrid network*.

Social Engineering

Social engineering attacks involve any way that a person can be deceived. Social engineering tests and attacks human targets. People can be fooled into giving an attacker too much information or granting them unwarranted access to a computer system. Pentesters who engage in social engineering must find out!

Phishing is when a cyberattacker pretends to be a trusted entity, like someone's bank or a company like Netflix, in order to maliciously acquire sensitive information. Phishing is most often done with fake websites, phony emails, and suspicious text messages. A common type of phishing attack is when a fake website is made to look like an ecommerce service in order to acquire the victim's username, password, and possibly credit card credentials.

Trojan malware pretends to be a file or application that a user wants, like a game or a photo attachment to an email, so that the victim will execute it.

Another type of social engineering attack involves contacting customers or employees through phone, email, or text while the attacker pretends to be someone else. This is a form of spoofing, otherwise known as an entity pretending to be something they're not. By pretending to be someone else, an attacker can acquire information that they have no right to have. "Hello, I'm Jason Smith, a customer at this bank. I forgot my password, please tell me what it is." Pentesters are often expected to spoof trusted entities to test an organization's resistance to social engineering attacks. It's vital to note, however, that any attempt to fool a company's employees must comply with the legal agreement between the pentester and the company itself. Otherwise, you could be charged with conducting fraud, which is obviously a clear violation of the criminal codes of all U.S. states and pretty much all countries worldwide! Cyberattackers often perform these sorts of social engineering attacks in order to do reconnaissance so that they can further penetrate the network that they're targeting.

A pentester often has to simulate social engineering attacks to figure out if customers or employees can be fooled by cyberattackers.

Physical Security

Physical security is a very important but often overlooked area of pentesting. Not only can computers and human beings be exploited by cyberattackers, but buildings can be as well. Attackers often want to have direct physical access to the computers they'd like to exploit.

Can an unauthorized person get inside a datacenter or server room? Can an unwelcome individual wander into an office and touch the PCs in people's cubicles? Those are the sorts of problems ethical hackers of physical security try to discover in their testing. And yes, pentesting sometimes involves crawling through ducts to get into datacenters!

Types of Pentesting

In addition to different areas of penetration testing, there are also different types of pentesting. The different types of pentesting refer to how much knowledge the ethical hacker has of the system they're hacking before they do their work.

Black Box Testing

In *black box testing*, the pentester has little to no knowledge of the system they're hacking. They truly have the perspective of an external cyberattacker. Deploying black box testing is useful for discovering if an external cyberattacker can penetrate your network or application.

A significant percentage of the cyberattacks that a real-life network faces each and every day come from ignorant external attackers. Sometimes, attackers deploy bots through the Internet, randomly looking for particular vulnerabilities to exploit. Sometimes, attackers don't have the time or motivation to do much reconnaissance work.

The advent of the dark web and its illicit markets have made external cyberattacks so much easier to deploy. For the cost of some cryptocurrency, potential attackers can buy exploit kits that can be used to develop malware to exploit specific systems or applications. Alternatively, for potential attackers who may have no computer programming ability whatsoever, they can buy malware that's already developed. For example, such individuals can purchase ransomware that maliciously encrypts data storage with the decryption key outside of the victims' hands, demanding a ransom payment for file recovery. Illicit cryptocurrency miners can use a tiny bit of computer processing power on a large number of CPUs in order to make an attacker money. Lots of other types of malware and exploits can be purchased on the dark web as well.

Because external cyberattacks are easier than ever to deploy, the information that a pentester can acquire through black box testing is really valuable.

White Box Testing

Whereas black box testing is done with little to no knowledge of the system being tested, *white box testing* is accomplished with pentesters having a lot of knowledge of what they're testing.

White box testers know all sorts of information about the system they're testing. They know which specific hardware and devices they're targeting, down to their particular models and configurations. They know which particular operating systems are being used, and which particular applications are being run on them. They also know identifying information like IP addresses, routers, and other networking details. Sometimes, they may even have the source code for the applications that they're testing.

Internal cyberattacks are definitely a thing. They're often deployed by disgruntled employees and contractors. These people frequently have user accounts with the networks that they intend to cyberattack. Moreover, they usually have knowledge of the systems that they want to attack, which can only be acquired by being an employee or contractor. Sometimes, internal cyberattackers are even information technology people or developers who are employed by the organizations they intend to attack. Their technical knowledge could be very advanced indeed!

White box testers simulate the role of an internal cyberattacker. And sometimes, white box testers have a better idea of which particular vulnerabilities to test for their exploitative weakness.

Gray Box Testing

You probably know that if you mix black and white paint, you get gray paint. So, if you assume that *gray box testing* is a mix of black box and white box testing, you'd be absolutely correct!

A gray box tester may know which operating systems are in the network and what kinds of devices are on it, but little else. Or, they may know that a web application was built with Joomla, but they might not know much else about it. In a nutshell, a gray box tester knows more than a black box tester, but less than a white box tester.

Gray box testing simulates an external cyberattacker who has gained illegitimate access to an organization's network infrastructure documents or has otherwise done some degree of reconnaissance of their target.

To pentest most effectively, organizations should hire ethical hackers to conduct black box testing, white box testing, and gray box testing as well. The knowledge acquired through these different methodologies is complementary.

A Brief History of Pentesting

As you start on your journey to becoming an ethical hacker, it would be useful to understand the history of pentesting as a discipline. An understanding of history always helps as you acquire a new area of expertise. History teaches us about the successes and failures of the past so that we can learn from mistakes and go with what works. As long as time is linear, the past always affects the present and future! A knowledge of computer science is important for understanding cybersecurity, but so is a grasp of the humanities. Frankly, the history of computing is fascinating, and knowing a bit of it will help you as a pentester.

The Early Days of Pentesting

1974 marked the birth of what most computer scientists consider to be the first microcomputer, the Altair 8800. This was considered to be the first personal computer, in retrospect, although the term was invented by IBM in 1981 with the advent of the IBM PC. When Steve Wozniak and Steve Jobs formed Apple Computers and launched the Apple I in 1976, their product helped to popularize microcomputers with computer hobbyists. Many vendors produced early microcomputers throughout the late 1970s and 1980s. These were the first computers that were practical for small offices and people's homes. In the 1980s, using a modem they could connect to early online services such as email and BBSes (bulletin board systems).

1984 was a pivotal year in the world of hacking. *2600: The Hacker Quarterly* debuted in January (www.2600.com). *2600 Magazine* readers would try hacks that they learned from the publication on early PCs and through early online services. *2600 Magazine* is still in publication today.

That same year, the first formal penetration tests were conducted by the U.S. Navy. The U.S. government started to crack down on "unlawful programmers," and the U.S. Navy wanted to test how accessible the computers on naval bases were to external hackers via early telecommunications services.

Improving the Security of Your Site by Breaking into It

Sir Tim Berners-Lee invented what was then known as the World Wide Web in 1989. It became available to the general public in August 1991, and we know it as the "web" today. People confuse the concepts of the web and the Internet. The web is simply one of many services that operate through the Internet.

The first proper whitepaper on ethical hacking was published by Dan Farmer and Wietse Venema in 1993, titled "Improving the Security of Your Site by Breaking into It," (fish2.com/security/admin-guide-to-cracking .html). The publication of this paper marked the genesis of penetration testing as a serious and formal area of study.

NOTE   The terms "pentesting" and "ethical hacking" have become a lot more common in the 21st century.

Farmer and Venema encouraged pentesters to read their paper on the web. By "site," the authors meant any online service such as a website, email server, or FTP server. Most important, the site had to be yours. You have the right to hack your own site, but you don't have the right to hack other people's sites without their permission, as that would be illegal cyberattacking. Farmer and Venema's paper established not only some of the basic methodology of pentesting, but also the pentesting ethics. These are the ethics that you must abide by in order to be an *ethical hacker*.

We encourage readers of the book to read the whitepaper, which is still freely available online. It's an important historical document that will inform your philosophy as a pentester.

Also, in 1993, Jeff Moss started the first DEFCON cybersecurity event in Las Vegas. The event grew each year, and nowadays the event attracts tens of thousands of people. Much of the discipline of ethical hacking is taught through the event, and the hundreds of similar cybersecurity events around the world are inspired by DEFCON, such as Security BSides and Blackhat.

Pentesting Today

Nessus is the first network vulnerability scanner, a type of application you'll use a lot as a pentester. Renaud Deraison started the project in 1998. By October 2005, Tenable Network Security purchased the project and made the software proprietary and commercial (www.tenable.com).

OpenVAS (www.openvas.org) developed as an open-source fork of Nessus for those who couldn't afford a Nessus license or otherwise wanted free software. Both Nessus and OpenVAS are still used frequently today.

Mark Curphey founded the *Open Web Application Security Project (OWASP)* in 2001 (owasp.org). OWASP focuses on pentesting web applications specifically. This nonprofit organization now has just over a handful of employees, but well over 10,000 volunteers. OWASP develops specific web application security testing standards and offers educational programs to the general public.

H.d. Moore started the Metasploit Project in 2003. Metasploit has become another popular network vulnerability scanning platform (www.metasploit .com). Rapid7 acquired the application in October 2009. As of this writing, Metasploit is available for free in its Metasploit Framework and Metasploit Community editions, or as paid software in the Metasploit Pro edition.

BackTrack was the first Linux distribution designed specifically for penetration testing (backtrack-linux.org). The first version of BackTrack was released in May 2006.

By March 2013, BackTrack was superseded by *Kali Linux* (www.kali.org). Offensive Security still maintains and develops Kali Linux today. You'll learn more about Kali Linux in Chapter 4 and Chapter 5. The Kali Linux operating system is full of useful penetration testing applications. It's free software that you'll be expected to use as a penetration tester!

Summary

Becoming a pentester requires that you develop a wide range of hacking skills. There are many ways to develop those skills, from conferences to educational programs to experimenting on your own computers at home.

The hacker mindset is the ability to think like a hacker and be able to find ways to exploit vulnerabilities. It takes more than technical knowledge to be an effective hacker; you need the right attitude! The hacker mindset is a culmination of creative and analytical thinking.

The Pentester Blueprint Formula is a combination of technology knowledge, hacking knowledge, and the hacker mindset. All three of these areas must be combined in order to be an effective ethical hacker, and it's the philosophy upon which this book is based.

The mediums of ethical hacking include operating systems, applications, networks, social engineering, and physical security. Sometimes, ethical hackers focus on just one of these areas. At other times, you will combine these facets.

The three basic types of pentesting include white box, gray box, and black box testing. White box testing starts with the amount of knowledge of a specific computer system that an insider, such as a network administrator, may have. Black box testing is conducted from the perspective of an external cyberattacker with little or no knowledge of a specific computer system. Gray box testing is somewhere in between, perhaps equivalent to a company employee who doesn't work in the IT department.

The history of pentesting is parallel to the history of computing and wouldn't exist without it.

Microcomputers and PCs started to appear in small offices and people's homes in the late 1970s and 1980s. PCs exploded in popularity in the 1990s, and this facilitated the tremendous growth of the Internet. But with many more computers in the world, accessible to ordinary consumers, cyber threats increased with the greater reach of computer technology. Now cyberattackers didn't need expensive academic or institutional computers. Computers became inexpensive enough for most households to have one, and they all became connected to each other through the Internet. Sadly, the Internet became a medium for cyberattacks like the world had never previously witnessed.

The first formal penetration testing was conducted by the U.S. Navy in 1984 in order to make sure that computers on their bases couldn't be penetrated by external hackers through the early online services.

Dan Farmer and Wietse Venema's 1993 whitepaper, "Improving the Security of Your Site by Breaking into It," helped to establish the ethics and some of the methodologies of pentesting that are still in use today.

The first proper cybersecurity conferences started in the 1990s. Nessus, the first network vulnerability scanning application, launched in 1998. Nessus, OpenVAS, and Metasploit are network vulnerability scanners that you'll likely use as a pentester.

The first operating system dedicated to pentesting, BackTrack, launched in 2006. Kali Linux replaced it in 2013. Kali Linux contains many ethical hacking applications, and you'll be expected to know how to use it in your ethical hacking career.

4 Education Resources

As you saw in the second stage of the Pentester Blueprint Formula, acquiring hacking knowledge is required. A lot of learning resources are available, and trying to figure out which resources to use can be tough, especially for those with no pentesting experience. You have different options when it comes to pentesting learning resources, and we will discuss them in this chapter.

Pentesting Courses

Pentesting courses are offered in some colleges and universities as part of a cyber security degree or certificate program. Most learning institutions offer one or two courses. At Richland College, for instance, Ethical Hacking (pentesting class) and Web App Pentesting are currently offered. Pentesting courses are also offered at conferences and through training companies. Some consulting companies that offer pentesting services provide basic pentesting training and some even offer advanced training. Some courses are CBT (computer-based training) or online. These course options are typically self-paced.

Training Companies
- SANS Institute (www.sans.org)
- Mile2 (mile2.com)

Online Training Companies
- SANS Institute (www.sans.org)
- eLearn Security (www.elearnsecurity.com)
- Pentester Academy (www.pentesteracademy.com)
- PentesterLab (pentesterlab.com)

In Chapter 6, "Certifications and Degrees," we'll explain in greater detail how to train for specific pentesting certifications.

Pentesting Books

Good books are available that address pentesting and ethical hacking. Books are good learning resources, and you can keep them on your bookshelf or phone and refer to them whenever you need to.

You already have this book—congratulations! Now, let's add to your collection. No one book can fully cover a topic as large as penetration testing. We frequently update our own libraries with books to learn new skills and to have as a reference. Books, like any self-study learning option, are going to be a more challenging way to learn. There's no instructor to ask questions, but you can get help online from other ethical hackers. Try social networking platforms like Twitter or LinkedIn to help answer your pentesting questions.

Here is a list of books that we recommend for expanding your pentesting education, from beginner to more advanced levels:

Penetration Testing: A Hands-on Introduction to Hacking (*No Starch Press, 2014*)
Georgia Weidman's book is a good companion to some of the content provided in this book. In addition to explaining how to use Kali Linux for the first time and run virtual machines with vulnerable operating systems, Weidman explains how to use Nmap, Wireshark, and Burp Suite.

She describes how to conduct simulated cyberattacks involving reconnaissance, finding exploitable vulnerabilities, bypassing antivirus software, and brute forcing passwords and wireless encryption.

We recommend that you combine Weidman's pentesting lab building tips with what you'll learn about in Chapter 5, "Building a Pentesting Lab."

Penetration Testing for Dummies (*For Dummies Press, 2020*)
Robert Shimonski's fine book is a new addition to the popular For Dummies series. Of course, you're not a "dummy," but if you're new to pentesting, then this book is especially useful. Never be afraid to admit that you're a noob!

In this book, Shimonski explains the various phases of a pentest from pre-engagement to completion. In every pentest, you must have a legal agreement with the owners of the network that you're targeting, with a well-defined scope. You do reconnaissance, and exploit vulnerabilities, and then you must write a detailed report explaining the vulnerabilities that your client must mitigate. Shimonski reviews the whole process for you. There's also quite a bit of information here about threat modeling and understanding risk from the perspective of your pentesting subject.

Penetration Testing Essentials (*Jones & Bartlett Learning, 2015*)
Sean-Phillip Oriyano's book is another great guide for beginning pentesters. There's a lot of useful content here that provides you with step-by-step tutorials, suggested exercises, and even downloadable exercise files!

Learn about information gathering, scanning, and enumeration techniques. Learn not only how to evade detection as you simulate cyberattacks but also how to cover your tracks afterward. These are all things that cyberattackers do, and you must learn how to imitate them.

This book will give you a lot of technical knowledge that you'll need to have in order to be an effective ethical hacker. It will help you to understand cryptography and system hardening concepts. There's also a useful guide to building your pentesting lab. Wow, between what you learn in this book and these other books, you'll probably have one of the best pentesting labs ever!

The Hacker Playbook: Practical Guide to Penetration Testing Series (*CreateSpace Independent Publishing Platform, 2015*)
This is a trio of books by Peter Kim that includes the following:

- *The Hacker Playbook: Practical Guide to Penetration Testing*
- *The Hacker Playbook 2: Practical Guide to Penetration Testing*
- *The Hacker Playbook 3: Practical Guide to Penetration Testing*

Obviously, we recommend that you read the books in order. Kim uses American football metaphors in his series. If you're an NFL fan, you'll really enjoy this. If not, maybe you'll be looking up terminology like "a play," "pregame," "drive," and "the lateral pass" on Wikipedia. That's how Kim describes the different phases of a penetration test.

Kim's series describes how to overcome pentesting roadblocks like various security controls and antivirus software. The third book is the red team edition, explaining pentesting from a red team perspective. If you're a pentester, you may become a red teamer one day. Red teamers often conduct pentesting, but they do so while working with an organization over a long period of time, crafting all kinds of offensive security campaigns to test a company's network over the long term. They also often emulate the tactics, techniques, and procedures (TTPs) of specific advanced persistent threat and organized crime groups.

Tribe of Hackers Red Team: Tribal Knowledge from the Best in Offensive Cybersecurity (*Wiley, 2019*)
As we mention in Chapter 5, the cybersecurity industry is a small world where many of us know each other! You enjoyed Marcus Carey's foreword to our book. Well, Carey and Jennifer Jin are the authors of the *Tribe of Hackers* series. To emphasize how small our world really is, Phillip Wylie is interviewed in *Tribe of Hackers Red Team*, and Kim Crawley is interviewed in the first *Tribe of Hackers* book.

We swear that we're not recommending *Tribe of Hackers Red Team* for the sake of our egos. But in addition to Phillip Wylie, this book also features interviews with many of the other stars of the offensive security realm, such as Jayson E. Street, Georgia Weidman (there's her name again!), Rob Fuller, David Kennedy, and many others. These interviews are worth reading for the same reason that the interviews in this book are so meaningful. These people have many years of experience in pentesting and other facets of red teaming, and it will benefit you to learn from those experiences as you prepare to become an ethical hacking professional yourself.

Penetration Testing: Security Analysis (*Cengage Learning, 2010*)
This book is from EC-Council Press. It's worth noting that EC-Council is a major certification body in the cybersecurity world. In Chapter 6, we mention EC-Council's Certified Ethical Hacker certification. *Penetration*

Testing: Security Analysis is a guide to the EC-Council Certified Security Analyst (ECSA) certification.

The ECSA is geared more toward general security analysts than people who just specialize in pentesting. But pentesting is a part of the ECSA curriculum, and there's a lot of useful content here, even if you're not pursuing the ECSA in the next few years.

This is one of the more advanced guides that we recommend, and it will also help you understand how pentesters can help security operations centers (SOCs) and chief information security officers (CISOs).

Unauthorised Access: Physical Penetration Testing for IT Security Teams
(*Wiley, 2009*)
In Chapter 2, "Prerequisite Skills," we mentioned how physical security is a facet of penetration testing. Pentesters don't just try to hack networks ethically by performing actions on their computers. Physical access is a major factor in the security of a network! Can a cyberattacker physically get into a server room by following authorized personnel (tailgating) into the building? Can a cyberattacker get into your office by crawling through the ducts? Are a building's physical locks breakable? Can security cameras catch people when they're up to no good?

These are all questions physical pentesters try to answer. You may very well be expected to try to penetrate a network physically in your work. Wil Allsopp's book covers the topic from the perspective of an IT security team. It's a useful guide for when you become a more advanced ethical hacker.

Allsopp's book includes social engineering, which is the art of fooling human beings. It also covers how to defeat locks, electronic keypads, and other electronic access systems. You'll learn how to hack security cameras. You'll understand how to do intelligence work with satellite imagery and in-depth information gathering. The book also covers planting bugs, hacking security cameras, and dealing with security guards. This book should really make you feel like a Hollywood hacker.

Advanced Penetration Testing: Hacking the World's Most Secure Networks
(*Wiley, 2017*)
This is another useful advanced pentesting guide by Wil Allsopp. In Chapter 5, we interview some pentesters who actually develop their own pentesting tools using their computer programming knowledge. This book

shows you how to do some of that stuff with VBA, Windows Scripting Host, C, Java, JavaScript, Flash, and other languages.

This book covers a lot of other advanced ethical hacking concepts as well. You'll learn how to do more network vulnerability testing than you can do with just Kali Linux and Metasploit Framework. You'll also learn how to discover and create attack vectors from scratch.

The book explains some advanced social engineering techniques, which use human psychology to exploit people who have access to the networks that you'll pentest. You'll learn about privilege escalation and how to breach networks, operating systems, and trust structures. You'll even learn how to acquire credentials maliciously in order to gain further access into your targeted network. When you're ready to learn more advanced pentesting techniques, this book will be especially useful.

Pentesting Labs

Hands-on experience is the best way to learn about pentesting, and building a pentesting lab is a must for any aspiring pentester. Building a lab can be an educational experience. "Learn to build, to learn to break" is great advice! When you learn how to install a web server, for example, you gain an understanding of how it works. You learn the web server directory structure as well as the other parts of the web server. You learn how to configure security on the web server as well as to see how security configurations can be exploited. Purposely vulnerable VMs (virtual machines) can also be used in your lab.

We explain pentesting labs and how to build them in a lot more detail in Chapter 5. We mention labs in this chapter as well, because they're a great educational resource! Your lab is where you'll learn by doing. You won't need to break the law by hacking unauthorized targets, because there are operating systems that you can virtualize and virtualized pentesting networks on which you can test your skills without harming anyone's real computer.

Web Resources

Websites that feature pentesting information and related news stories are a perfect complement to all of the books that we recommend for you to read.

Here are some of our favorite websites for you to check out. The great thing about the web is that these resources are dynamic. The best websites are worth visiting again and again because their content will grow as time goes on. Make sure to bookmark these sites in your favorite web browser!

Daniel Miessler (danielmiessler.com)
Daniel Miessler has worked in the cybersecurity industry for over 20 years. His writing and commentary have appeared in many corners of the media with which you may be familiar, such as *Forbes*, *The Wall Street Journal*, *CNBC*, *The A Register*, and *Fortune Magazine*.

Miessler has a podcast called "Unsupervised Learning," and the site has links to its episodes. You can also sign up for his newsletter.

There's a wide range of tutorials on Miessler's site covering topics like DNS, information security metrics, Big Data, obscurity, Shodan, and lots more. You'll spend many hours with them.

His site also features his blog and links to his many YouTube videos. In our opinion, Miessler's site is one of the best online pentesting information sources, especially if you enjoy acquiring knowledge in many different forms.

Penetration Testing Lab (pentestlab.blog/log)
This blog is regularly updated as of this writing. New posts are published approximately once every couple of weeks. Posts are organized in a variety of categories including social engineering, mobile pentesting, general lab notes, exploitation techniques, and coding. Here are a few of our favorite posts on this site:

Phishing Windows Credentials
(pentestlab.blog/2020/03/02/phishing-windows-credentials)

This blog post covers using C#, Metasploit, and Windows PowerShell to acquire usernames and passwords in networks that use Windows Server and Windows 10. These are the most popular operating systems in office environments, so what you learn here will be useful in a lot of your pentesting work.

Using Metasploit to Create a WAR Backdoor

(pentestlab.blog/2012/08/26/using-metasploit-to-create-a-war-backdoor)

This guide is for more advanced web application pentesting. A backdoor allows an external cyberattacker to acquire internal access to their target. You'll learn to simulate more complex web hacks in this post.

Pen Testing SQL Servers with Nmap

(pentestlab.blog/2013/04/21/pen-testing-sql-servers-with-nmap)

This blog post shows you how to do something really cool with a tool you'll already have in your pentesting lab. SQL servers drive the backends of a lot of the web applications and online services that you use every day. Finding SQL server vulnerabilities is really sophisticated stuff! There's a lot of harm a cyberattacker can do if they acquire malicious access to a SQL server, such as a breach of sensitive financial data!

You will need to install a SQL server on your own computer or use a virtual pentesting network like Proving Grounds (mentioned in Chapter 5) to try the exercises in this post.

So You Want to Be a Pentester? (jhalon.github.io/becoming-a-pentester) When dancing only causes embarrassment, give pentesting a go! Jack Halon lists a large number of useful resources that you can use to explore pentesting further. Jack also provides an overview of some of the technical skills that you'll need to have as a pentester.

Web app security is very important! Chances are that today you've already used some web apps—Facebook, Twitter, Amazon, and so on. A lot of the big data breaches in the news that you'll hear about are from exploited web vulnerabilities:

- Network security encompasses securing networks of connected computers. The Internet is one massive network, but homes, offices, and industrial plants have their own internal networks as well.
- Code review is a way to find software vulnerabilities in computer programming code. This code manifests as everything from scripts, to applications that you run in your operating system, to the operating systems themselves, and to web applications.
- Binary reverse engineering is another way to find software vulnerabilities. Reverse engineering an application is a way to extract the code that it's made of.

Halon also covers hardware and embedded devices security. Hardware is the physical aspect of our computers and computing devices. Embedded computers are found in everything from ATMs to elevator systems, from industrial plants to vending machines. Basically, they're the computers that are inside the things we use that exist as machines that don't present themselves as computers.

Halon also covers Amazon Web Services, mobile security, and pentester education programs.

PentesterLab Blog (`blog.pentesterlab.com`)

This is a Medium-hosted blog that's operated by PentesterLab. Every few months, there's a new post that's full of insight. We recommend that you explore the blog's older articles, too.

Here are some of our favorites:

Invest in QA!
(`blog.pentesterlab.com/invest-in-qa-509082217904`)

This article explains why companies should spend time and money on quality assurance teams in their application development. If applications are security-tested before they're deployed in production environments, a lot of vulnerabilities and cyberattacks can be avoided!

i/ considered harmful
(`blog.pentesterlab.com/i-considered-harmful-6e20936ea65f`)

This article explains an important web app security concept. Websites sometimes try to get their URLs (web addresses) included in lists of trusted URLs. A lot of malware and cyberattacks act through the web, so website and web application allowlists can be very useful. Sometimes, web developers use the "i" expression to avoid the tedium of putting URLs on an allowlist, one by one. This article explains why that can be dangerous.

Four Easy Capture-the-Flag Challenges
(`blog.pentesterlab.com/easy-capture-the-flag-challenges-698db5d67309`)

This article explains some exercises people can try when they design their own Capture the Flag (CTF) competitions. CTF is a type of hacking game where you explore an application or network to "capture" a flag, such as a script or a line of code. We explain CTF competitions in more detail in Chapter 8, "Gaining Experience."

Summary

This book is an excellent first step on your journey to becoming a pentester. While you're on your way, there are also many other means to expand your knowledge and become a better ethical hacker.

Companies like SANS Institute, eLearn Security, Pentester Academy, and PentesterLab offer online pentesting training programs that we encourage you to try.

There are many books that you can buy, in both physical and ebook formats, that you can read and add to your reference collection. Our favorites include *Penetration Testing: A Hands-on Introduction to Hacking*, *Penetration Testing for Dummies*, *Penetration Testing Essentials*, *The Hacker Playbook: Practical Guide to Penetration Testing* trilogy, *Tribe of Hackers: Red Team*, *Penetration Testing: Security Analysis*, *Unauthorised Access: Physical Penetration Testing for IT Security Teams*, and *Advanced Penetration Testing: Hacking the World's Most Secure Networks*.

Build a pentesting lab that includes your computer and a lot of useful ethical hacking applications. Experimenting with penetration testing techniques on your own equipment is one of the best ways to learn. Chapter 5 explains building a pentesting lab in greater detail.

There's also a lot of great web content that will teach you a lot about pentesting. Our favorite sites include Daniel Miessler's website, Penetration Testing Lab, So You Want to Be a Pentester?, and the PentesterLab Blog.

5

Building a Pentesting Lab

Having a lab is a good way for pentesters to test exploit code and other types of simulated cyberattacks. Testing a proof of concept (PoC) prior to using an exploit during a pentest can enable a pentester to ensure that the exploit will work in production. Some exploits can make systems unstable, and testing it in a lab is a good way to verify the safety of the exploit.

Whether you're learning the craft of ethical hacking or doing work as a paid professional, having your own pentesting lab is a must.

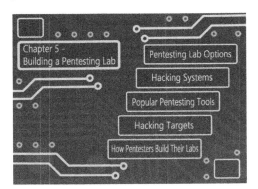

Chapter 5 –
Building a Pentesting Lab

Pentesting Lab Options

Hacking Systems

Popular Pentesting Tools

Hacking Targets

How Pentesters Build Their Labs

Pentesting Lab Options

You have options when it comes to building your lab. You can take a minimalist approach, or you can build very complex labs. The more complex you get with your lab, the longer it takes to set up.

The choice you make may depend on the amount of time and money you want to invest. You can build your lab using routers, switches, personal computers (PCs), and servers. Something to consider with complex labs is that the more complex the lab, the more electricity it will consume as well as the more heat it will output, which may also result in using more electricity in order to cool the area where your lab is located. Complex labs can also be noisy due to the system components, such as the internal fans used to cool the computers.

Minimalist Lab

This option is less costly and requires less electricity to operate. It can be a single computer running multiple VMs. The attacking system OS can be the host OS, or you can use a VM dedicated to hacking with target VMs to hack. This option could be set up on a laptop, which would make your lab portable.

A portable lab allows you to study in different locations. Sometimes, changing study locations allows you to study longer. Changing up your study environment can also help hold your interest longer. A portable lab allows you to study at work on your lunch break or to take it with if you must travel.

An ideal minimalist lab could be just a laptop computer with Kali Linux installed on it. The laptop provides portability, so you can test physical networks on the go. Kali Linux contains hundreds of different pentesting applications. Your most frequently used applications would probably be Metasploit Framework for network vulnerability testing, Wireshark for packet analysis, and Nmap, so that you can look at how the various networks to which you connect are configured. There's also a Wi-Fi cracking suite that includes Aircrack-NG and a few other apps, which is useful for whenever you need to test WEP or WPA2-protected wireless networks. You may want to carry an Ethernet cable to connect your laptop to wired networks and a USB thumb drive for putting files onto computers or taking files from them.

Dedicated Lab

This option is the next step up from the minimalist lab. For a dedicated lab, you have separate computers for your attacking system and the hacking target system. This option adds a networking element to your lab because the target systems and the attacking system are not contained on a single device. You can have more than one computer for your hacking targets.

Your dedicated lab will likely be a desktop or laptop PC with Kali Linux installed on it that you keep in your own office most of the time. In addition to USB thumb drives and Ethernet cables, you will also have your own ISP service, which you can use for testing networks remotely through the Internet. It may be more useful to work from your own location when you don't need direct physical access to the network that you're testing, and you need to run applications such as network vulnerability scanners for more than eight hours at a time. Your dedicated lab will enable you to perform tasks that would take longer to finish than your laptop's battery can handle on one charge if you're on the go with your minimalist lab.

Advanced Lab

This is the most expensive of the three options, and it requires the most electricity. This option is more complex to configure, and it takes more to maintain.

If you run into problems with your lab, it can be time-consuming to troubleshoot. The benefit of this option is the learning opportunities. Configuring and networking multiple systems is a great learning experience, and the advanced lab option can be as complex as you desire. With this option, you would build an attack system and hack target systems, and the attack and target systems are networked together. You can use routers and switches, which can be separate hardware devices or virtual using Pfsense (www.pfsense.org), an open-source firewall software distribution based on the FreeBSD UNIX-like operating system.

An advanced lab can include a laptop with Kali Linux that you take with you when you travel, a laptop or desktop PC with Kali Linux parked in your office with your own ISP connection, and some extras. The extras can include routers, switches, or Pfsense; some Hak5 devices, such as a Shark Jack and a Wi-Fi Pineapple; and a virtualization client, such as Oracle VirtualBox. There are multiple uses for your virtualization client. You can install VMs of operating systems on which you can test malware, and you can install vulnerable disc images from places like VulnHub to try to exploit specific vulnerabilities. Virtual machines are explained in the next section.

Hacking Systems

A pentester uses a computer to perform pentests and hack targets. You can install hacking tools directly on your computer or in virtual machines. You can find preinstalled tools on pentesting Linux distributions or scripts like the Pen Tester Framework (PTF) by TrustedSec (www.trustedsec.com), and you can install pentesting tools on Windows using FireEye's Commando VM (virtual machine) script (github.com/fireeye/commando-vm).

As you know, operating systems are the software that your computer needs in order to run applications. Examples of operating systems include Windows or macOS on your computer, or iOS or Android on your smartphone. We will be describing Kali Linux, an operating system that was specifically designed for penetration testing.

What's a *virtual machine (VM)*, you might ask? Well, instead of just running directly on a physical computer, an operating system can also run as an application within another operating system. You need a computer with an operating system, and then you need software for running operating systems as applications. For that, you'll need virtualization software, such as Oracle VirtualBox (www.virtualbox.org). Let's say, for example, that you are running Windows on your PC. You can install VirtualBox in Windows, and then install macOS in VirtualBox. Basically, you can configure VirtualBox to pretend that it's a Mac and run macOS on it. That's the wonder of virtualization!

Virtualization has many uses for pentesters. Is there malware that you want to test without it doing harm to a real computer? You can do this by executing the malware in a virtual machine. If the malware is so harmful that it makes your virtual computer impossible to use, you can just uninstall the virtualized operating system with no effect on the OS that's running directly on your PC.

There may be many different types of cyberattacks that you'll want to simulate without doing harm to any real computers. Virtual machines make this possible.

Popular Pentesting Tools

There are thousands of different applications that pentesters use. Which applications you use will depend on the types of networks, computers, and applications that you will be ethically hacking. The following is a summary of some of the most common applications that pentesters use.

Kali Linux

Kali Linux is perhaps the most fundamental pentesting tool available. It's a complete free operating system that you can install directly on your PC or run as a live DVD without installing it on your hard drive. You should definitely visit the Kali website to download a disc image that you can burn onto a blank DVD (www.kali.org).

Some of the tools that are already installed in Kali include Nmap, Wireshark, Sparta, Metasploit Framework, Maltego Teeth, and WebSlayer. Kali Linux has many, many more tools, and it may take you years to explore all of them fully. As we explain in Chapter 6, "Certifications and Degrees," Offensive Security, developer of Kali Linux and certification authority for OSCP, has its own certifications that are specifically geared toward using Kali Linux professionally.

Nmap

Nmap (nmap.org) stands for *network mapper*. If you run Nmap on a network that you're testing, you can see how it was designed and how it operates. Nmap includes host discovery for seeing which network services servers run, port scanning to see which TCP/IP network ports are running on those servers, and operating system detection so that you can see which OS servers and clients are in use on the network.

Wireshark

Wireshark (www.wireshark.org) is a packet analyzer. *Packets* are the sections of data that computers send to each other through a network. All data sent through a network is sent in the form of packets. For instance, when you run a web browser on your PC, your PC (the client) sends packets to a web server requesting a web page and then the web server sends your client packets containing the data that makes up the web pages you visit. With Wireshark, you can see what those packets contain if they aren't encrypted! If an online service was foolish enough not to encrypt your financial data when you buy something online, a cyberattacker could use Wireshark to see your credit card number. Scary stuff, eh?

Vulnerability Scanning Applications

Metasploit Framework, Nessus, and OpenVAS are all network vulnerability scanning applications:

```
www.metasploit.com
www.tenable.com
www.openvas.org
```

In these programs, you can configure your computer to try exploits for specific operating systems, web applications, and the applications that are run on client machines and servers. If any of the exploits work, you have then found known vulnerabilities that you can report as a pentester.

A common misconception is that pentesting is just running these network vulnerability scanning applications. However, a network vulnerability scan is just one part of a proper pentest. Plus, there's some work and professional knowledge that's needed just to use a network vulnerability scanning application properly! Nothing about pentesting is as simple as it looks.

Hak5

Hak5 (shop.hak5.org) makes a number of different devices that are designed for pentesting. Shark Jack (shop.hak5.org/products/shark-jack) can be plugged into a network to run thorough reconnaissance on it. USB Rubber Ducky (shop.hak5.org/products/usb-rubber-ducky-deluxe) can be used to install backdoors and acquire sensitive data like usernames and passwords. (It's not as cute as it sounds!) Wi-Fi Pineapple (shop.hak5.org/products/wifi-pineapple) can be used to exploit vulnerable wireless networks. Hak5 has many more physical devices that can be very dangerous in the hands of a cyberattacker but very useful in the hands of an ethical hacker.

Hacking Targets

To develop hacking skills, you need targets to attack. Obviously, attacking other people's computers without their permission is a massive, illegal no-no. Instead, you can build your own vulnerable systems, which is a very educational experience. If you don't have the time to do this, however, you can download vulnerable VMs for your lab.

PentestBox

PentestBox (pentestbox.org) is a wonderful free pentesting target on which you can test your ethical hacking skills.

PentestBox can be especially useful as a testing environment because it's designed to run directly in Windows without the memory and CPU requirements of a virtual machine. It can also spare you the hassle of switching between operating systems on a multiboot computer. A *multiboot computer* has more than one operating system directly installed on its hard drive, with a different partition for each operating system.

PentestBox allows you to run malware and other simulated cyberattacks while sandboxing them from the Windows operating system that's directly installed on your computer. Give it a try!

PentestBox is a convenient system on which to run experiments because you can install it directly in Windows without having to run it in a virtualization client like Oracle VirtualBox.

VulnHub

VulnHub (www.vulnhub.com) is a large and growing collection of vulnerable VMs that you can install in virtualization clients like VirtualBox or VMWare. Contributors create operating systems and applications with particular vulnerabilities that you can find. The last time we checked, there were hundreds of different VMs that you can try on your own computer through this website. This resource is definitely worth checking out for its variety of ethical hacking targets.

Proving Grounds

Offensive Security has its own virtual pentesting network, Proving Grounds, which you can try to hack (www.offensive-security.com/labs). Proving Grounds includes a modern Windows domain structure, Linux production environments, Active Directory (for administrating Windows clients), and attack simulations, such as file server attacks, man-in-the-middle attacks, privilege escalation, and buffer overflow attacks. Keep in mind that Proving Grounds is a paid service. If you truly want to become a professional ethical hacker, however, Proving Grounds Teams Edition can be a worthwhile investment if you share the expense with friends who are also learning about penetration testing. It's definitely something that's worth checking out.

How Pentesters Build Their Labs

Before you start building your own pentesting lab, it may help you to learn how other successful people have done it. We asked some people in the industry about their pentesting labs. Hopefully, you will get some ideas and be inspired!

Chris Kubecka is notable in the cybersecurity industry for restoring Saudi Aramco's network from one of the world's most destructive cyberwarfare attacks in 2012. We asked her how she built her pentesting lab.

Chris Kubecka

"I prefer using a locked down Windows or Linux-based operating system that will be compatible with the target. Kali is not setup secure, which means it can leave it open to attack. Most of my engagements in-person have discovered an attacker already present. The tools in Kali are not set up with security in mind, using default ports, default credentials, or have their own known exploits. Nmap, for instance, has several in-built scripts that can be used to exploit a default configuration Metasploit instance. If your pentest has collected private, critical data, or health data, you, as the tester, can be a wonderful point of an attacker. That is why it is important to secure your pentesting system, even if you use Kali.

I incorporate IT, web application, IT networking, IoT [Internet of Things], and ICS [industrial control systems] with encryption and hash deciphering. Included are aspects of technical social engineering and things like attacks through a browser using JavaScript and attacks against browsers like collected passwords stored in plain text once a target machine is acquired and the browser can be attacked. Lastly, metadata tools. These require additional tools.

FOCA is a metadata tool that looks at documents, pictures, presentations, and so on. It can sift through the hidden metadata and map out internal networks, external networks, show which software versions are in use, usernames, passwords if present, printers, lots."

Why did she design her lab that way?

"The big why is out of necessity. Kali is great, but it is constrained by known vulnerabilities and exploits. It is also based on IT systems, not IoT and ICS for the most part. If Metasploit has an exploit in its library, great. If it doesn't, no. Some of the known exploits in various Kali tools may also have low chances or perform poorly in a system versus Metasploit modules that are graded 'great,' which are the opposite. Once you learn how exploits work, what the scripts are doing, you can write many exploits with multiple programming languages. You can also expand them. For instance, an exploit might be known to work against Vendor version X, but you learn that other vendors use the same vulnerable library that can be exploited, but either in the same or a slightly different way."

An anonymous person told us about their lab. We don't know why they prefer to be anonymous. We know their identity, but it's important to respect someone's privacy if they request it. Here's what they told us about their tools.

Anonymous 1

> "I built all my own tools. I built network packet crafting, hard drive recovery, self-modifying executables."

Like Chris Kubecka, our anonymous source clearly has a lot of computer programming know-how. Network packets are the data we send over networks, such as the Internet. It sounds like they were making them from scratch!

> "Much of my research was on client-side applications, security control systems."

A client-side application is pretty much any sort of application your PC uses. Clients, otherwise known as endpoints, are the computers we use to interact with networks. Your PC and phone are common types of client machines.

> "I built targeted payloads for pivots."

A payload in malware is the part that does the actual damage to an infected computer. For instance, a ransomware's payload starts the work of maliciously encrypting a victim machine's files.

> "I built my own reverse engineering tools in C#. Everything I wrote was on Visual Studio."

Reverse engineering an application is taking it apart to look at its computer programming code.

> "I created application injection payloads to move and pivot around a computer. It got baked into a Metasploit payload. I released my source code hidden in a puzzle only people who loved to crack applications would find."

So, an application injection payload is the part of malware that gets inside a vulnerability in an application in order to do harm to a computer. And by hiding their source code in hacker puzzles, our anonymous hacker sounds like a mysterious character in a cyberpunk novel. Fascinating!

Simon Bennetts

Simon Bennetts told us a story about his pentesting lab and how it was useful for him.

> *"In 2009 I was a Java developer and team leader. I led a small team which developed an online service for a major accounting software company. As this service was considered to be security critical, I insisted that an external pentest team was hired to ensure the software was suitably secure.*
>
> *I remember walking into the room in which we'd set up the pentesters after just one hour to check they had everything they needed, only to find one of them logged into our admin console as me. We had only given them test credentials, and they already had admin access to the system! In this particular case, it was not my service that was at fault, they had in fact cracked the whole company's Single Sign On system!"*

That's impressive! And kind of scary.

> *"The final report, when it was delivered, looked like a car crash. I've since found out that it actually wasn't that bad and have now written much more damning reports myself. However, it also included vulnerabilities that I'd never heard of, including Cross Site Request Forgery."*

A cross-site request forgery happens when a user is authenticated into a web application and a cyberattacker hijacks their session to perform unwanted actions within the application. For example, let's say that you were logged in to your Facebook account in your web browser. Facebook is a web application in which you are authenticated. A cyberattacker exploits your session to make spam posts under your account, advertising some sort of scam. Attacks like that are possible through the kinds of web vulnerabilities that you may find as a pentester.

> *"I realized that I knew less about web security than I thought and that I needed to learn a lot more very quickly. The pentesters pointed us to OWASP, which I'm afraid to say I'd never heard of, and so I started with the OWASP Top Ten before moving on to some of the other OWASP guides. While the guides were very good, I find that I learn best by doing things rather than just reading about them, so I started playing around with various open source security tools.*

I've always had side projects, but at that time I had never contributed to open source. I decided it was a good time to start contributing, so looked around for an open source security tool with an active community. Unfortunately, I couldn't find one. OWASP had WebScarab, but I didn't really get on with that, and in any case development on that seemed to have stopped.

The tool I most liked was called Paros Proxy. It was simple, effective, and did what I needed. It was also written in Java, so it wasn't long before I pulled in into Eclipse [an application for developing in the Java programming language] and started making some tweaks.

I found that other developers and QA people at the company were also somewhat lacking in security knowledge, so I started giving talks on the OWASP Top Ten."

Simon explained further about the tools he has used.

"I decided to do a proper investigation. I wanted the tool I recommended to be free, opensource, and cross platform. It needed to do all of the basics but didn't have to be a hardcore pentesters' tool. Ideally it would also have an active community."

So, in layperson's terminology, he wanted a tool that has source code that's available to the public, which can work within multiple operating systems and web browsers; hence, open source and cross-platform.

"I couldn't find anything that met those criteria. The closest tool was Paros, or rather the version of Paros I was hacking around with! I took the plunge, forked Paros, renamed it ZAP, and announced it on BugTraq. I also proposed it as an OWASP tool and was actually very surprised when it was accepted a couple of months later.

ZAP was always intended to be a community tool, and since its release hundreds of people have contributed to it. It's now managed by a core team and has become the world's most frequently used web application scanner."

That's incredibly impressive. He built a web application scanner that became the most popular application in its category!

Jason Wheeler

Jason Wheeler isn't a full-time pentester, but he often pentests in his work.

"Lately, a lot of my work can't be discussed as it's pending, but I can still talk about methodologies and tools used. I hack on a wide range of topics from web applications, hardware hacking, phone apps, to finding weaknesses in cryptography (implementation mostly). You name it, I most likely dabbled in it, except for social engineering, which I'm not very good at yet.

As far as my lab goes, it's quite extensive. My personal lab has one bare metal server [a server which just runs an operating system directly, no virtual machines] with 1080 Ti GPUs for hardcore math-ing, 4 hypervisors with multiple full-blown networks from Windows 7 to Server 2019, IDS (intrusion detection system), and SIEM (security information and event management, a special system for detecting cyberattacks).

My lab is always changing to fit what I am currently researching. Also use ZeroTier to connect networks together to share resources or I alternate to a VPN for red team games we host. My work lab is quite large, but I'm limited on what I can say about it."

The pentesters we've spoken to have so many secrets! We asked another anonymous person how they built their pentesting lab.

"Our lab started simply as a network we conducted our remote activities from, as well as a network that was used to conduct recon-naissance against our targets—host discovery, host enumeration and host banner grabbing. We did not have commercial tools that were able to meet our operational requirements and (like most) built it in-house. The only commercial tool we were able to incorporate into our operations was CORE IMPACT, which was used to initial access and after which we would upload our in-house devel-oped implant."

So far, we've spoken to some of the world's top ethical hackers. Computer programming and application development knowledge will be useful to you as a pentester. Fortunately, as you start your pentesting journey, you won't be expected to develop your own tools from scratch. For the first several years of your career, being able to use applications other people have developed should be satisfactory. But maybe one day you will develop some of your own pentesting applications! Until then, maybe you will use some of the applications the pentesters we've spoken to developed. Once you get into the cybersecurity industry, you will find it's a very small world!

We asked another anonymous pentester about the tools they use and why.

Anonymous 2

"We used Nmap, CORE Impact, and that's about it. We did reverse engineer and clean up a lot of public exploits and then re-use them, but as a 'tool' in the common sense, we used mainly in-house development.

Operations followed the common methodology of Recce, enumerations, exploitation, expand and secure access, actions on network, clean-up, and get out."

Recce is military terminology for reconnaissance work.

"Automation and tools allowed us to have a measurable and repeatable process. These two key aspects helped set us apart from our peers in that we were able to show change over time for our clients. We could compare them to others in their industry. With our ability to store and database, we could quickly seize the initiative when new RCE (remote code execution) was available because we knew from our saved data which clients were exposed."

Remote code execution is what it sounds like. Someone has a computer, and they're executing code on a different, remote computer.

Ted James

Ted James specializes in web application security.

"In the early 90s, I was working as a technical writer for a software company that had us writing using an SGML variant. [Standard Generalized Markup Language is kind of like webpage development code, but for various types of documents.] A few years later, when the Web became a thing, I realized I already knew how to write HTML. [HTML is the main language web pages are written in.] I just needed to learn the tags. I built a few sites for some projects I was working on and ended up creating an intranet for my division at work. I had a lot of fun experimenting and dissecting existing sites and apps to learn how they worked and figure out how I could apply the functionality to my own sites. I 'appropriated' and modified a lot of great code in the process. Flash forward many years and many job changes. My first job in information security was as a technical writer for a team of penetration testers."

Ted described how he got into pentesting.

"When I was finally able to move into a full-time information security position, my new boss asked me what I wanted to learn to help me in my job. I told him that I wanted to learn penetration testing, so he bought me the eLearnSecurity Penetration Testing Student course. I picked up some great skills and knowledge, including creating a penetration testing lab with Kali Linux. My agency (state government) needed someone to test our new and existing web applications, so I jumped on the opportunity."

He explained his specific web application hacking tools.

"We were already using Nessus, but we upgraded to Tenable.IO. The upgrade included Tenable's Web Application Scanning (WAS). I run both credentialed and non-credentialed scans. For credentialed scans, I use Selenium scripts. I found a great browser plugin (Selenium IDE) for that. WAS is also perfect for creating site maps. When testing applications, it's necessary to map out all possible attack surfaces.

I use OWASP-Zed Attack Proxy (ZAP) for both passive and active scanning. ZAP is really an amazing tool in that it contains so many functions. It's also fully open source and community driven. If I need to intercept traffic, I can use it as a proxy. Otherwise, I really love ZAP's Manual Explore option. I love how it lets you explore an application, collecting vulnerabilities along the way. It's also perfect for creating Cross-Site Request Forgery (CSRF) proofs-of-concept."

Oh wow! We just spoke with ZAP's developer, Simon Bennetts! Ted continued to explain another of his tools.

"I use the Burp Suite Community Edition as a proxy when I need to intercept and manipulate web traffic and to map applications."

Pete Herzog went into detail when he described his pentesting lab. Hopefully you'll find this information useful!

Pete Herzog

"The lab has two parts: a front and back end. The front has the tools and the back has the servers. Even though we made it much more complicated over the years to accommodate AI mentoring and VR, the design is still the same."

Artificial intelligence and virtual reality? Cool stuff!

"I think most labs now are made with Docker or some other virtualization for easy spin-up and static configuration. The static part is so it can be reset, important if you do any scoring in a CTF or requiring it to be broken for a pentest class or even a virtual escape room.

The tools we focus on in-depth for our certification classes are:

- Ping: Hping3
- Traceroute: Tcptraceroute
- Netcat
- OpenSSH
- Nmap
- Dig, Whois, DNSLint
- Wireshark, TCPdump
- Burp

The students are free to experiment and try all the other tools in Kali or Parrot (another pentesting operating system) or whatever, but what we want them to know is the basis of how the tool works and what it's doing."

BLuef0x

Finally, we asked BLuef0x about how they started and their pentesting lab.

"I started by going to HackMiami meetings and conferences back in 2018, as well as DC813 and The Undercroft meetups. There I made friends with fellow hackers who talked and showed me various tools for pentesting, as well as network defense. Also, I started going online using YouTube to do virtual schooling, and I self-taught on setting up my lab at home, which I built. My time in the army also showed me how basic InfoSec systems worked, both internally and externally.

The first tools I learned were Nmap and Wireshark. These tools are a powerful combination where they are used to analyze a basic entry into a network, a server, or even standalone terminals. Now, assume your location is okay with using Nmap and the destination of the scan, you can begin to find out more about the target. Wireshark helps with finding out more about how and who the target is talking to such as websites, types of requests for information, or access to a site. Wireshark can be used on wired and wireless connections. So, gathering info about the target using both Nmap and Wireshark alone can tell you how the target operates. Another tool I use is social engineering where I would gather information about a target by talking to other people who are associated with the target."

We think this really reinforces how important Nmap and Wireshark will be when you explore networks as a pentester.

Summary

Having your own pentesting lab is useful for both learning about ethical hacking and conducting ethical hacking work as a paid professional.

Your lab will consist of the hardware and software you use to simulate cyberattacks.

Your main lab hardware will be your PC. Hak5 also makes a number of small devices that can be plugged into physical networks to simulate specific cyberattacks.

Using the Kali Linux pentesting operating system is a must for pentesters these days. Kali can be installed directly on your PC, or you could run it off a DVD without installing it onto your hard drive.

Some of the tools that are found in Kali Linux that are frequently used by pentesters include Nmap for exploring networks, Wireshark for looking at the data packets that are sent to and from computers through networks, and Metasploit as a network vulnerability scanning tool. OpenVAS and Nessus are other popular network vulnerability scanners.

Obviously, as you learn the craft of ethical hacking, you cannot target other people's computers without their consent. Instead, there are applications that you can run on your own computer to use as your hacking targets.

PentestBox is a vulnerable cyberattack target application that you can run in your Windows PC. VulnHub is a website where you can download a wide variety of vulnerable virtual machines that you can run in a virtualization client as a target for you to attack. Offensive Security also offers Proving Grounds, a paid service that gives you a virtual network in which you can simulate cyberattacks.

The pentesters whom we've spoken to in this chapter use many of the tools that we've mentioned. Some of them have even developed their own software for penetration testing use!

6

Certifications and Degrees

Certifications and degrees can be helpful for people trying to get into pentesting as well as other areas of information security, and having these credentials is especially helpful when you have little to no experience in the employment field that you are pursuing. Opinions differ, however, on the need for degrees and certifications—there are skilled and successful pentesters both with and without degrees or certifications.

Such credentials are not a substitute for pentesting knowledge or skills. With or without certifications or degrees, job applicants will have to go through an interview process and, in some cases, a hands-on technical assessment that tests their pentesting skills. Regardless of the direction you choose to go, make sure that you understand the technology rather just relying on your credentials or memorization.

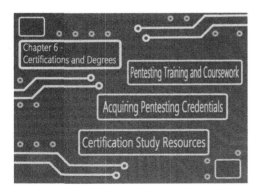

Pentesting Certifications

You have options when it comes to pentesting, and some non-pentesting certifications could still be helpful for aspiring pentesters. Some certifications are well-known with pentesting while others are not. The well-known certifications are typically the ones with which human resources and management are familiar. These pentesting certifications are what we refer to as entry-level credentials.

Entry-Level Certifications

Certified Ethical Hacker

EC-Council's *Certified Ethical Hacker (CEH)* certification is one of the first ethical hacking certifications and probably one of the most useful ones for finding a job as a pentester. The CEH is a Department of Defense (DoD)–recognized certification, and it is part of the DoD Directive 8570 certifications. The CEH can be helpful in getting government contracts.

EC-Council prefers that you have two years of pentesting experience before taking the exam, but you can get a lot of that experience from simulating cyberattacks on virtual machines, virtualized networks, and your own devices, as described in Chapter 5, "Building a Pentesting Lab." As of 2020, the current version of the CEH is v10. When taking the exam, you are given four hours to conduct your 125-question exam in a supervised environment and, at the time of this writing, it costs $1,199 USD to take. Here are the modules on the exam to get you started:

- Introduction to Ethical Hacking
- Footprinting and Reconnaissance
- Scanning Networks
- Enumeration
- Vulnerability Analysis
- System Hacking
- Malware Threats
- Sniffing
- Social Engineering
- Denial-of-Service
- Session Hijacking
- Evading IDS, Firewalls, and Honeypots
- Hacking Web Servers
- Hacking Web Applications
- SQL Injection
- Hacking Wireless Networks

- Hacking Mobile Platforms
- IoT Hacking
- Cloud Computing
- Cryptography

PenTest+

CompTIA's A+ and Network+ were some of the first IT certifications (www .comptia.org). Though EC-Council has a number of certifications that are specific to cybersecurity, CompTIA is the vendor-neutral certification body that's probably best known for covering all of the major areas of IT in general.

Given the increasing demand for experienced penetration testers, CompTIA created the *PenTest+* certification and launched it on July 31, 2018. It is one of the newest pentest certifications. The PenTest+ learning materials do a great job of covering pentesting methodology and pentesting itself. PenTest+ is a great starting point for those wanting to learn about pentesting.

If you're working on your EC-Council CEH, it would probably be a good idea to get this certification, too. But if the CEH's $1,199 price tag is a bit overwhelming for you, you can go for the PenTest+ certification first. It's relatively inexpensive at $359 USD, at the time of this writing. You will be given 165 minutes in a supervised environment to answer a maximum of 85 questions on the exam. There are no mandatory prerequisites, but it's recommended that you have a CompTIA Security+ certification and three or four years of information security experience.

eLearn Security Junior Penetration Tester

The *eLearn Security Junior Penetration Tester (eJPT)* certification is offered by eLearn Security (www.elearnsecurity.com). eLearn Security certifications and learning content are online, hands-on material. The eJPT, as well as other eLearn Security offerings, require a practical exam including a pentest to be conducted as part of the exam process. eLearn Security certifications may not be as widely known as some others, but they have great learning content.

Intermediate-Level Certifications

Offensive Security Certified Professional

The *Offensive Security Certified Professional (OSCP)* certification is the product of Offensive Security, a pentest consulting firm and the creator of the popular

Kali Linux penetration testing operating system (www.offensive-security
.com/pwk-oscp). The certification exam requires that you take a 24-hour practical pentest exam. To pass, you must hack into targets on the network and
must score 75 or higher. This certification is highly sought after by companies
who are hiring pentesters.

As a pentester, you'll hear about Offensive Security a lot. The organization
is also a certification body, and it offers many certifications that can be useful
in your pentesting career. The Offensive Security Certified Professional is
probably the first certification you'll want to get, but only go for it after you've
acquired EC-Council's CEH, CompTIA's PenTest+, or both, as the OSCP is an
intermediate certification, rather than a beginner one.

Penetration Testing with Kali Linux is where you should start. It's Offensive
Security's own course to prepare you for the OSCP exam. The course covers
the following topics:

- Getting Comfortable with Kali Linux
- Command Line Fun
- Practical Tools
- Bash Scripting
- Passive Information Gathering
- Active Information Gathering
- Vulnerability Scanning
- Web Application Attacks
- Introduction to Buffer Overflows
- Windows Buffer Overflows
- Linux Buffer Overflows
- Client-Side Attacks
- Locating Public Exploits
- Fixing Exploits
- File Transfers
- Antivirus Evasion
- Privilege Escalation
- Password Attacks
- Port Redirection and Tunneling
- Active Directory Attacks
- The Metasploit Framework
- PowerShell Empire
- Assembling the Pieces: Penetration Test Breakdown
- Trying Harder: The Labs

Offensive Security lets you buy the PWK course and the OSCP exam at the same time. At the time of this writing, the course and exam combination is $999 with 30 days of lab access, $1,199 with 60 days of lab access, and $1,349 with 90 days of lab access. You can sign up for these packages on Offensive Security's website.

GIAC Penetration Tester

Training for the *GIAC Penetration Tester (GPEN)* certification is offered by the SANS Institute (pen-testing.sans.org/certification/gpen) and the exam governing body is GIAC (www.giac.org/certification/penetration-tester-gpen). This is a hands-on class that teaches students the tools, techniques, and methodologies used by pentesters. The content is created and taught by some of the most well-known experts in the field. The exam for this certification is a proctored, question-based exam. This certification is highly sought after by companies who are hiring pentesters.

Advanced-Level Certifications

Offensive Security Certified Expert

If you have your CEH, PenTest+, and Offensive Security's OSCP certification, what's next? Why don't you go for the Offensive Security Certified Expert certification, Offensive Security's most advanced pentesting exam? It's a real challenge!

The *Offensive Security Certified Expert (OSCE)* certification (www.offensive-security.com/ctp-osce) is from Offensive Security, like the OSCP. The OSCE content teaches advanced pentesting skills and exploit development. Like the OSCP, the OSCE exam uses a practical lab exam that requires pentesting and exploit writing. It is a 48-hour exam. This certification is highly sought after by companies who are hiring pentesters.

Cracking the Perimeter is Offensive Security's course to prepare you for the OSCE exam. Here are some of the topics that it covers:

- Cross Site Scripting Attacks
- Directory Traversal / LFI Attacks
- Backdooring PE Files
- Advanced Exploitation Techniques
- ASLR
- Egghunters

- Exploit Writing (Zero-Day Approach)
- Attacking Network Infrastructure
- Bypassing Cisco Access Lists Using Spoofed SNMP Requests
- Sniffing Remote Traffic via GRE tunnels
- Compromising Router Configs

You absolutely should have your OSCP before you even consider the OSCE. The OSCE, however, could give you a real edge in being hired as a pentester! As with the OSCP, you can buy the Cracking the Perimeter course and the OSCE exam at the same time. The cost with 30-day lab access is $1,200, and with 60-day lab access, the cost is $1,500. Everything you need to know is on Offensive Security's website.

GIAC Exploit Researcher and Advanced Penetration Tester

The *GIAC Exploit Researcher and Advanced Penetration Tester (GXPN)* is offered by the SANS Institute, and it is an advanced pentesting skills certification (www. sans.org/course/advanced-penetration-testing-exploits-ethical-hacking). The certification is similar to the OSCE, and it teaches exploit development and advanced pentesting. The exam for this certification is a proctored, question-based exam. This certification is highly sought after by companies who are hiring pentesters.

Specialization Web Application Pentesting Certifications

GIAC Web Application Penetration Tester

The *GIAC Web Application Penetration Tester (GWAPT)* is a web application pentesting certification offered by the SANS Institute (www.sans.org/course/ web-app-penetration-testing-ethical-hacking). The exam is a proctored, question-based exam. This certification is highly sought after by companies who are hiring pentesters.

eLearn Security Web Application Penetration Testing

The *eLearn Security Web Application Penetration Testing (eWAPT)* certification (www.elearnsecurity.com/certification/ewpt) is offered by eLearn Security, and it requires that you pass a practical pentest exam like the other eLearn Security certification exams.

Offensive Security Web Expert

So now you have your OSCP certification, and you really want to specialize in hacking websites and web applications. You may want to study for the Offensive Security Web Expert certification next. The web is a big part of our everyday lives, and it is a significant cyberattack surface! So, OSWE could be a useful specialization to have.

The *Offensive Security Web Expert (OSWE)* certification is offered by Offensive Security, and it is an advanced web application pentesting certification (www.offensive-security.com/awae-oswe). The course used to prepare for this certification is Advanced Web Attacks and Exploitation (AWAE). It's Offensive Security's course to prepare you for the OSWE exam. Donovan Cheah wrote about his experience with the AWAE course on his blog:

> "The AWAE incorporates different programming languages, databases, and web application vulnerabilities. The web vulnerability classes include blind SQL injections, cross-site scripting, and deserialization. Throughout the course, scripting skills are emphasized. Exploits aren't good enough; we sometimes try harder by automating them. Be comfortable in a scripting language of your choice. Python is excellent since the course is in Python, but it is alright to use another scripting language of your choice.
>
> Since this course is a white box penetration testing course, it introduces different methods of debugging, such as simply writing console.log() statements to print output in JavaScript and dynamic debugging in .NET with dnSpy (dnSpy is awesome; even if you don't plan to take the AWAE, take some time to reverse engineer a .NET application). A white box penetration tester must be familiar with walking through code execution flows with the help of a debugger. The AWAE will be about 50% of the time on a debugger, about 20% of the time spent scripting, and if you try harder, 30% on the extra miles and other research."

As is Offensive Security's style, you can buy the AWAE course and the OSWE exam at the same time from its website. At the time of this writing, with 30-day lab access, the fee is $1,400; with 60-day lab access, it's $1600; and with 90-day lab access, it's $1,800.

Wireless Pentesting Certifications

Offensive Security Wireless Professional

Once you have your OSCP, you may choose to specialize in hacking wireless networks. Wireless networks are a big deal these days! They exist everywhere from your home WLAN to big corporate offices. They present a massive cyber-attack surface that can penetrate mobile devices, PCs, and servers alike.

Offensive Security Wireless Attacks (WiFu) is Offensive Security's pentest-ing and certification course to prepare you for the *Offensive Security Wireless Professional (OSWP)* exam (www.offensive-security.com/wifu-oswp). Like the other Offensive Security certification exams, this one is a practical, hands-on, lab-based exam.

These are some of the many topics that are covered in the WiFu course:

- IEEE 802.11
- Wireless Networks
- Packets and Network Interaction
- Linux Wireless Stack and Drivers
- Aircrack-ng Essentials
- Cracking WEP with Connected Clients
- Cracking WEP via a Client
- Cracking Clientless WEP Networks
- Bypassing WEP Shared Key Authentication
- Cracking WPA/WPA2 PSK with Aircrack-ng
- Cracking WPA with JTR and Aircrack-ng
- Cracking WPA with coWPAtty
- Cracking WPA with Pyrit
- Additional Aircrack-ng Tools
- Wireless Reconnaissance
- Rogue Access Points

Like with all of Offensive Security's other programs, you can buy the WiFu course and the OSWP exam simultaneously. They can be purchased together from Offensive Security's website for $450.

GIAC Assessing and Auditing Wireless Networks

GIAC Assessing and Auditing Wireless Networks (GAWN) (www.sans.org/course/wireless-penetration-testing-ethical-hacking) is offered by the SANS Institute and goes beyond Wi-Fi to cover software-defined radio (SDR), Bluetooth, Zigbee, near field communication (NFC), and radio-frequency identification (RFID). The exam is a proctored, question-based exam.

Mobile Pentesting Certifications

Mobile Application Security and Penetration Testing

The Mobile Application Security and Penetration Testing (MASPT) certification covers mobile application security and pentesting. The exam is a practical, hands-on lab requiring exam candidates to perform a pentest. This certification is offered by eLearn Security, and you can learn more about it by visiting their website at www.elearnsecurity.com/course/mobile_application_security_and_penetration_testing.

GIAC Mobile Device Security Analyst

The GIAC Mobile Device Security Analyst (GMOB) certification covers mobile application security and pentesting (www.giac.org/certification/mobile-device-security-analyst-gmob). The exam is a proctored question-based exam. This certification is offered by GIAC, which is its own certification body.

Pentesting Training and Coursework

Most information security disciplines have degree choices that are directly related to those roles, but the academic path of a pentester is less concrete. Pentesting-specific degrees are hard to find at the college and university level. Some degree programs offer pentesting, but these courses are more commonly referred to as "ethical hacking."

The SANS Institute offers a master's degree in information security. SANS offers courses that focus on pentesting. But as all information technology and computer science knowledge is useful to pentesters, acquiring general information security and computer science credentials can be time well spent.

As discussed in earlier chapters, technology and information security knowledge is needed by pentesters. Computer science degrees are also helpful to aspiring pentesters. The programming skills taught in computer science courses are helpful for exploit development and pentest tool creation.

Acquiring Pentesting Credentials

A number of different certifications and degrees can be useful in the pursuit of employment in your pentesting career. Getting credentials will help show both employers and clients that you understand the theory and practice of ethical hacking and other areas of cybersecurity. Some employers may even insist that you have specific certifications or degrees in order to qualify for the roles they're seeking to fill.

When you plan your path for acquiring the credentials as you start your pentesting career, there are a lot of decisions that you'll have to make. It will be very helpful if you do some research beforehand to determine which credentials are most worth your efforts. Be prepared to invest a lot of time and money in acquiring these certifications. Your investment, however, will prove truly worthwhile for your career.

PENTESTING AND RED TEAMING SCENARIOS

The following documents the personal experiences and benefits of acquiring credentials of several individuals with well-established pentesting and red teaming careers.

Andy Gill

Andy Gill took some time to find his pentesting career path, and he studied for his degree after an internship:

> "I got into the industry via a sort of standard and non-standard path. During high school, I, unfortunately, failed all of my exams in my last year, which led to me winging it. I went to college to study computer networking on a two-year course. However, along the way I managed to land myself an internship at a bank working with their technology and information risk team, where I quickly found that it wasn't for me and I much more enjoyed the red and blue team side of things.

Following this internship, I managed to get into university, and I picked up a degree in Digital Security, Forensics, and Ethical hacking which I leveraged to get involved with the cybersecurity challenge. It was the first step near the industry that I was able to make. My first job after the bank internship was as an intern at a security company. That's where I found my taste for hacking and learning the ropes."

Sebastian Mora

An internship was instrumental to Sebastian Mora's career as well.

"In my junior year of high school, my school offered its first computer science course. I learned more about programming and how computers worked, which grew my interests further. For one of my projects, I wrote a program that could print across all the printers on the network, abusing open FTP ports and no network segmentation. The school didn't find it as amusing as I did!

Once I graduated, security got put on the back burner as I didn't think it was a real career path. I applied for the Computer Science program at San Jose State University and began focusing on becoming a software engineer. About a year ago I began searching for internships. That's when I stumbled upon a red team internship in Pleasanton. While it was a fairly junior red team, my manager and coworkers were very supportive and always pushed me to learn and research. That internship opened my eyes to the professional world of information security. Later that year I went to DEFCON [a popular cybersecurity convention].

If you're not in your teens or twenties anymore, don't worry about it! Many pentesters didn't start their ethical hacking careers until they were older. Sometimes the professional experience people attained in different industries and roles became useful in their pentesting careers later on."

Steve Campbell

Steve Campbell could be considered to be a late bloomer, and still his ethical hacking work thrives.

"I took the long route to getting into pentesting and didn't get into it full time until I was in my late forties. I first became interested in computers while serving in the U.S. Navy as an Aviation Electrician. I also liked detective and mystery novels, and liked snooping into things that were "forbidden," which led to hacking. I got in trouble a few times for digging a little too far into computer systems at work. At my last duty station before I retired, I was pulled into the IT shop and became the system administrator when they found out about my passion for computers.

Around the same time, I found my first vulnerability by snooping around the URL printed at the bottom of a Navy form. I discovered an IDOR [Insecure Direct Object Reference] which exposed the PII (personally identifiable information) of hundreds of thousands of Marine Corps and Navy personnel to the Internet. I was scared to report it and thought I'd get in trouble, but I went ahead, and they didn't make a big deal out of it. I eventually found that they remediated it by configuring Internet Explorer to not print the URL at the bottom of the page! I completed my bachelor's degree in Computer Information Science with a concentration in Networking and Security Management at East Coast Polytechnic Institute.

After retiring from the Navy, I wanted to get an information security job but no longer wanted to deal with government bureaucracy. So, I got a non-cleared job in IT and let my [security] clearance expire. I worked as a Network Technician and Systems Engineer for eight years. I earned various certifications including CCNA, CCA, and Security+. Then one day while studying for an IT certification, I had the realization that the only thing that I felt any passion for learning was hacking. I had to force myself to learn anything else. That's when I heard about Offensive Security's OSCP certification. I passed it on the first try at the age of forty-six. My employer didn't have any interest in creating a full-time security position on the team, so I found a new job as a security engineer for a hospital where I occasionally got to do penetration testing. I left that job to become a Security Analyst IV and lead an application security team for a very large corporation."

The moral of Steve's story is that there are many different routes to a successful pentesting career, and it's never too late!

Martino Dell'Ambrogio

Martino Dell'Ambrogio also took a while to discover that pentesting was the right career for him.

> *"I first heard of the profession in 2007, from a judge who suggested I apply my self-acquired knowledge in offensive security this way instead of just having fun in order to satisfy my curiosity but to avoid getting in trouble. I was given a contact at the local security firm by him, which later I found out was one of the first doing this kind of job in Western Europe. But I wasn't yet sufficiently confident in my knowledge to apply.*
>
> *I didn't know about any related certifications or degrees then, but the judge was also a law professor and one of his students based his master's degree on my story. At least I knew someone in the academic world was interested.*
>
> *I was hired as a security analyst in a SOC [security operations center] service shortly after, where I got a GIAC Intrusion Analyst certification to add to my Swiss Computer Specialist apprenticeship. Up to this point, I had always thought that I would—and that I wanted to—become a developer, but I discovered I was good in the business side of security as well.*
>
> *The company I was working for had a pentester and didn't need another one, or didn't believe I could do it. In 2009, I finally applied for a pentester role at the security firm. The contact I was given wasn't around anymore, but they believed in me.*
>
> *I did get the Certified Ethical Hacker and Offensive Security Certified Expert later on, mostly to present my profile to prospects with something they know, before they actually know me. I also believe, sadly, that certifications are essential to those who have more difficulty presenting themselves as technical experts because of biases towards young people, women, minorities, and other oppressed groups."*

That's an excellent point. Perhaps certifications are especially useful to those from marginalized groups.

Rachel Tobac

Rachel Tobac's pentesting career has gotten her some major attention. She's even made appearances on American television through *Last Week Tonight with John Oliver* and *CNN*. Tobac explained how she got to specialize in red teaming and social engineering.

> *"My path to information security and pentesting is pretty nonlinear. I didn't go to school for information security. In fact, I have a degree in neuroscience and behavioral psychology! My neuroscience and behavioral psychology degrees help me understand how and why people make the decisions they do, which helped me down the line understand how to successfully hack those human systems when I got started in the field of social engineering.*
>
> *I got my start social engineering in the DEFCON Social Engineering Capture The Flag (SECTF) and studied for years from the social engineering masters to learn everything I know now. Chris Hadnagy taught me the concepts and skillsets for social engineering through his books, podcasts, Social Engineering Framework and mentorship, and I also got super helpful advice from @_sn0ww, @cgsilvers, @HydeNS33k, and so many more experts in the field. After that, I started social engineering my service providers to see what information I could gain access to (legally) without authenticating myself properly.*
>
> *After a lot of self-study and social engineering practice, I ended up getting second place three years in a row in the SECTF competition, and I joined the board of Women in Security and Privacy (WISP). From there, I started speaking about my experience in social engineering at small meetups and events. Companies then started to reach out for me to educate their teams based on my experience hacking, and then I got asked to start doing penetration tests for those organizations. Now I have my own company, SocialProof Security, and we do social engineering training, live hacking demos, workshops, talks, and penetration tests. Due to COVID-19, we now lead all of these trainings, workshops, talks, and pentests remotely, and I miss the travel but love getting to spend more time with my dog at home.*

In terms of certifications, many folks find certifications helpful in leveling up their experiences and communicating their expertise. And I think they do help communicate that level of expertise for many people who may be historically overlooked in the hiring process. I've been lucky to have the three SECTF experiences under my belt to communicate my experience, and my client recommendations helped after that. Instead of spending my time on certifications and degrees now, I spend my time trying out new attacks and testing new vulnerabilities in human systems with clients and my service providers. I have found that the easiest way for me to get good at hacking systems and protocols fast is to do it as often as possible—many people learn well in a classroom or educational setting, but I tend to learn the skills best by trying them out."

Tinker Secor

Sometimes people are lucky enough to have their experience speak for itself instead of having to acquire certifications. Tinker Secor's path to success is a fine example of that.

"I messed around with computers and hacking in high school. I joined the U.S. Marine Corps after 9/11. After I got out of the USMC, I did odd jobs. It was 2008, and I took what I could get. I worked in IT Recruiting for a couple years and got back into computers. Then I decided to get into information security. It made good use of my approach and mentality from the Marines and my old experience from high school.

I joined the Dallas Hackers Association, gave firetalks (short talks on hacking), networked, and became an intrusion detection analyst for a Security Operations Center of a large company. I detected and stopped hacking attempts against our enterprise. I did that for a couple of years. At the Dallas Hackers Association, I was approached by a burly pentester named 'Bubbles' and was asked to join their team. After a bit, I agreed and became a pentester.

I didn't have any certifications. I did have a liberal arts degree in history. My collegiate work focused on group dynamics, from the individual and small group on up to systemic movements. The analytics experience that I gained while writing history theses directly translated to the analytics work conducted while doing security ana-lytics. My military background also helped out, both in networking and in analytic and pentesting approach. The 'attack mentality,' they call it."

Thomas Hughes

Getting credentials that are specific to pentesting and other cybersecurity roles, such as the OSCP and the CISSP, can seem like an overwhelming endeavor when you're just getting started in your career. Don't lose hope! Thomas Hughes has been working as a pentester for years, and he had to take his OSCP exam twice.

"I began pentesting professionally while working in security architecture as a political science student. When a colleague was working on a problem in Fiddler, I joined in. Later, I went back to university for a year of computer science and found it very easy because I'd been building and breaking software for fifteen years already. I finished all of the first- and second-year courses in two semesters.

Looking at my straight As and how many jobs were available, I didn't see the immediate return on investment in finishing the computer sci-ence degree, so I found work at a local security company, Cloakware. Cloakware developed software used for control flow flattening and binary obfuscation. When I interviewed there, all I knew was that I wanted to work in a low-level programming language. Joining the security team, I got my wish and worked mostly on firmware reverse engineering, but I also started sinking my teeth into CTFs.

To get ahead in security, I realized I would need software development experience. I joined a ten-person startup just as they were finalizing their series B funding, and I worked there for two years. I was writing Python and JavaScript mostly, and pushing security left across the company as it grew. After that I returned to pure security work and ended up a pentester based on my CTF experience.

After two years as a pentester, I decided to pursue certs to try to make my employer happy. This meant that I had to get CSSLP and

OSCP. I tried OSCP first and failed. This made me panic, so I went back and did the CSSLP. I passed easily. So, the next month I did CISSP. Then my boss suggested I should also get CISA, so I did the month after. To capitalize on the momentum, I booked OSCP a week after that, and passed that easily too this time."

If you fail your first exam for a certification, it doesn't mean that you're not smart or that you don't have what it takes to be an effective pentester. You just might have to study more—and perhaps get some more hands-on experience. With further learning, consider writing your exam again. Some of the best pentesters in the industry faced hurdles while trying to acquire certifications.

Dominique Brack

Many pentesters had other information technology roles before they considered ethical hacking for a living. All experience with computer technology is a useful starting point for becoming a pentester. Dominique Brack acquired a lot of useful experience in different IT areas before studying for pentester certifications.

"Pentesting encapsulates a lot of different and complex topics from risk management to enterprise architecture, network, and endpoint security. My path was from hardware to security to pentesting. Once I felt competent enough in networking, PCs, and server OSes, as well as enterprise architecture, it was a small step to pentesting. When I started in IT and security, there had been no special programs or degrees around security, just general IT. I have a general degree in IT and several industry certifications, which all helped along the way. Most helpful for pentesting might have been CISSP, CISA, then Certified Ethical Hacker and Ethical Hacker Instructor, and then of course conference attendance like Blackhat and DEFCON groups."

Certification Study Resources

A lot of pentesters in the job market have managed to find work without certifications. But these days many companies insist that their pentesting new hires have some certifications under their belt.

Following are some books and online services that can help you prepare to take exams for the certifications that are the most in demand for pentesters. These are great resources that will help you ace your exam on your first try!

CEH v10 Certified Ethical Hacker Study Guide

This study guide is written by Ric Messier and was published by Sybex in 2019. It's a comprehensive guide that explains what you'll need to know to understand the questions that will appear in the various modules of the CEH exam.

EC-Council

Go straight to the source! The EC-Council website (www.eccouncil.org) is another great resource. This site has an entire section dedicated to the CEH certification that you won't want to miss. It has some useful documents in PDF format including a handbook; its own CEH blueprint (very clever!); an exam FAQ; a one-page guide on ethical hacking from home, which nicely complements Chapter 5 of this book; a course outline; and information about your various training options including iLearn self-study, iWeek online instructor-led training, a master class, and in-person training. Of course, you can also register for your training and schedule your exam through the site.

Quizlet CEH v10 Study Flashcards

These flashcards can be helpful in memorizing the terminology and concepts that you'll be learning as you prepare for the CEH exam. The flashcards are available for free on the web. So, if you learn best by repetition, it's a great web application for you to check out.

Hacking Wireless Networks for Dummies

This book is written by Kevin Beaver and Peter T. Davis and was published by the For Dummies press in 2005. WPA3 didn't exist when this book was published. Nevertheless, most of the wireless technologies we still use today are covered in this useful guide. It should certainly help you prepare for the OSWP exam. Some of the many topics covered in this book include the following:

- Hacking wireless clients
- Denial-of-service attacks
- Encryption cracking

- Wardriving
- User authentication

CompTIA PenTest+ Study Guide

This study guide is written by Mike Chapple and David Seidl and was published by Sybex in 2018. It will prepare you for everything and anything that'll appear on the exam. Beyond the book itself, you can also buy CompTIA PenTest+ Practice Tests at the same time! We strongly recommend that you do so.

CompTIA PenTest+ Website

This website (www.comptia.org/certifications/pentest) is also strongly recommended for preparing for the PenTest+ certification. Of course, you can also purchase the exam from the site. The site also has eLearning, exam prep, study guides, virtual labs, video training, and instructor-led training resources, whichever suits your learning style.

Cybrary's Advanced Penetration Testing

Cybrary's Advanced Penetration Testing course (www.cybrary.it/course/advanced-penetration-testing) is taught by Georgia Weidman. Given the hands-on nature of much of the PenTest+ exam, Weidman's course is very helpful. The course's modules cover Linux, programming, Metasploit, information gathering, vulnerability discovering and scanning, traffic capture, exploitation, passwords, advanced exploitation, post exploitation (that's a lot of exploitation!), web apps, exploit development, and the smartphone pentest framework. You can sign up for the online course on the Cybrary site.

Linux Server Security: Hack and Defend

This book by Chris Binnie, published by Wiley in 2016, isn't specific to the OSCP or Kali Linux, but it will help you a great deal, as you should understand the Linux hacking topics covered in the book in order to reach your full potential with Kali Linux and the OSCP exam.

Advanced Penetration Testing: Hacking the World's Most Secure Networks

This book, written by Wil Allsopp and published by Wiley in 2017, covers the sort of expert-level ethical hacking areas that the OSCE exam will expect you to understand, even though the book isn't specific to the OSCE or Kali Linux. Here are some of the advanced concepts covered in this book:

- Using Java applets for malware payload delivery
- How security operations centers work
- Windows PowerShell
- Hijacking DLLs
- North Korean networking technologies
- Asymmetric cryptography
- IDS evasion
- VBA attacks

The Web Application Hacker's Handbook: Finding and Exploiting Security Flaws

This book is written by Dayfdd Stuttard and Marcus Pinto, and the second edition was published by Wiley in 2011. The knowledge contained in this huge book is still relevant today, and it will help you a great deal in your preparation for the OSWE exam. It covers many topics, including the following:

- HTML5 exploitation
- SQL injection
- HTTP parameter pollution
- Cross-domain integration techniques
- JavaScript exploitation

Summary

There are many different paths that you can take to become a pentester. A few are very lucky to get hired without any formal credentials. But you should probably focus on learning everything you can about information technology and target certifications that are specific to pentesting. Not only does learning some theory help with your ethical hacking practice, but certifications are also a way to demonstrate to prospective employers that you have the knowledge they need.

Vendor-neutral certifications demonstrate specific information security knowledge without being tied to a technology vendor's products or services. Vendor-neutral certifications that employers often look for in their pentesters include EC-Council's Certified Ethical Hacker, CompTIA's PenTest+, eLearn Security Junior Penetration Tester, eLearn Security Mobile Application Security and Penetration Testing, GIAC Penetration Tester, GIAC Exploit Researcher and Advanced Penetration Tester, and GIAC Mobile Device Security Analyst.

Offensive Security develops the popular Kali Linux pentesting operating system. As a pentester, you need to familiarize yourself with Kali as it contains many useful applications for ethical hacking that you'll use on the job. Offensive Security also offers certifications that are based on understanding and using Kali. Their certifications are highly valued by employers. Offensive Security's certifications include Offensive Security Certified Professional, Offensive Security Web Expert, and Offensive Security Wireless Professional.

7 Developing a Plan

The prerequisites to learning pentesting and the hacking skills needed to be a pentester have been covered in Chapters 2, 3, 4, and 6. Everyone who becomes a pentester starts a little differently! Some people come to ethical hacking from IT and computer science backgrounds. Others have worked in restaurant kitchens, schools, medicine, law—or even as Uber drivers or daycare workers—you name it, and pentesting is their first foray into IT! Whatever your background, you will need your own custom road map personalized to your skills and needs.

In this chapter, we'll cover doing an inventory of your current skills and perform a skill gap analysis in order to create your action plan. You'd be surprised which of your many professional experiences can be useful in your new career as a pentester!

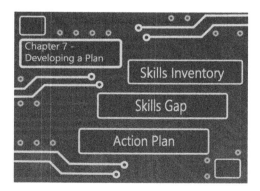

Skills Inventory

To start the process of building your own personal education plan, you need to create a list of things that you know and a list of topics that you need to learn more about and then compare them in a gap analysis to build your education plan. Table 7.1 can be used as a starting point to take inventory of your skills.

Table 7.1: Skills Inventory

Skill	Yes	No
Windows		
Linux		
Networking		
Security		
Scripting		
Active Directory (AD)		
Web Technologies		
Wireless Technologies		
Internet of Things (IoT)		
Hacking		
Web Hacking		
Wireless Hacking		
Social Engineering		
Physical Pentesting		
Android		
iOS		
macOS		
Firewall Configuration		
Python		
Java		
Reverse Engineering		
Antivirus		
Firewalls		
Critical Thinking		
Talking to Businesspeople		
Empathizing with End Users		
Creativity		
Perseverance		

The majority of these skills are related to computing. However, the last five listed are more subjective in nature and are likely to be skills that you acquired from outside the IT world. This is especially true if you replace "empathizing with end users" with "empathizing with customers." *End user* is just computer nerd jargon for the customers of computer technology, whether at home or in a workplace.

PROFESSIONAL EXPERIENCE SCENARIOS

Let's use our creativity to describe some possible scenarios of professional experiences that adults and teenagers might have before they consider a pentesting career. These examples should help you extrapolate your own life experiences in order to figure out which transferable skills you already possess.

Subject A

Marco runs his own little independent record label on Bandcamp. He engages in web development in order to maintain his own Bandcamp site on a dedicated subdomain. (A *subdomain* is the part of a URL that goes before the main domain name. In `www.google.com`, `www` is the subdomain. In `shoes.retailstore.eu`, `shoes` is the subdomain.)

Marco also interacts with customers who buy physical and digital recordings. He works with recording artists to come up with album cover art that pleases them, and he screens for third parties who may try to scam him.

Web development is a skill that's transferable to pentesting in obvious ways. Being able to develop web pages and web apps, and understanding how web servers and TLS certificates work, can be directly applied to pentesting web applications. Plus, some of that knowledge helps when it comes to understanding how other Internet services work, and how other application development languages and technologies work.

Marco's other skills are transferable to pentesting in less obvious but equally valuable ways. Interacting with music customers can be applied to interacting with your customers as a pentester. As a pentester, your customers are the companies that hire you to pentest their networks. You need to sell them on how you can help to make their networks more secure and to focus on fulfilling your services in a way that makes them happy and satisfies your legal agreements with them.

Working with recording artists to come up with album cover art that they like is helpful here as well in terms of satisfying customers. Finally, his experience in screening possible scam artists who target his small indie label can help him understand how cyberattackers use social engineering to exploit networks.

Subject B

Aisha works in a tech support call center. Her CompTIA A+ and Network+ certifications helped her get the job. This particular tech support call center provides support both over the phone and through remote connections. It's possible for Aisha's computer to connect to a customer's computer over the Internet so that she can see what's on the customer's display and to provide mouse and keyboard input into the customer's computer as if she were working on it directly. All shift long she takes calls and opens tickets for customers with issues ranging from network connectivity problems to malware to problems with using a particular application.

Aisha is also an exceptional writer. When she writes about what happens in each of her tickets, her coworkers understand her notes better than the ones written by her other coworkers. However, Aisha would like to earn more income, and all of the malware that she has removed remotely has piqued her interest in cybersecurity. Perhaps a pentesting career is right for her.

Which skills does Aisha have that could be transferable to a pentesting role? As you read in Chapter 2, "Prerequisite Skills," Aisha's A+ and Network+ certifications, plus her everyday work as a tech support specialist, have given her an excellent understanding of how PCs and computer networks work. These facets of computer technology are very often the subject of pentesting. Aisha remotely connects to customers' computers with their consent. But if the customers didn't consent, those remote connections could be part of a cyberattack!

As a pentester, Aisha needs to determine if the computer systems that she's testing will allow unauthorized remote connections, as that would constitute a significant security vulnerability. Did you know that a lot of Windows ransomware enters its targets through unsecured Windows Remote Desktop Protocol (RDP) connections? That's the sort of vulnerability that Aisha should be able to spot.

Sometimes, as a pentester, Aisha may also remotely connect to computers with consent in order to scan for vulnerabilities in their operating systems and applications. All that malware removal experience is also very valuable.

Aisha may deploy disk images of the operating system configurations for her pentesting clients' use in order to create virtual machines (VM). She could use those VMs to run malware to see if she can find vulnerabilities that way, similar to the work a malware researcher performs. Fixing the damage done by malware in her tech support job also gives Aisha an understanding of how her pentesting clients could apply the vulnerability information she gives them. Working with customers gives Aisha patience and social skills that are useful when working with pentesting clients, too.

Aisha's writing talent is another useful skill. She could use this skill to write vulnerability reports that her clients find easy to understand and apply. It's not enough to understand a subject well; communicating your ideas effectively is also very important.

Subject C

Jin is an HVAC technician. HVAC stands for heating, ventilation, and air conditioning. HVAC is very important when it comes to keeping homes and workplaces comfortable and functional. Jin works in a datacenter for one of the largest tech brands in the world, so his job is vital to keeping thousands of racks of servers cool enough to operate properly. A desktop computer needs to have a fan on top of its CPU and additional fans inside its case so the hardware components don't overheat, but rackmount servers produce much more heat than a simple PC! Multiply that by thousands of server machines, and even though the machines contain fans on the inside, their surrounding environment needs to be kept as cool as the inside of a refrigerator.

HVAC requires a lot of technical skills to maintain these systems, repair them, and keep them operating well. In a commercial or institutional environment like Jin's workplace, there are also many technical standards with which his HVAC system must comply.

Jin has so many skills that are transferable to his upcoming pentester career! He knows his way around and through the ductwork of a datacenter. When ethical hackers test physical security, they need to see if a determined cyberattacker can use the ducts to enter a datacenter without authorization. A determined adversary may try to crawl through ducts if their target servers are as valuable as the ones in Jin's current workplace.

Jin also understands a bit about the other physical security controls in a datacenter, such as doors, mechanical locks, and security cameras. All of this knowledge will help him a lot in performing physical pentesting tasks.

Jin's current workplace also has administrative security controls with which he is acquainted. Receptionists and security guards watch to make sure that only authorized personnel enter the datacenter. Not all of the people who are authorized to enter the datacenter are employees with whom Jin is familiar. Sometimes, electricians require access, and a lot of the cleaning staff come and go.

Jin understands how cyberattackers can socially engineer receptionists and security guards into believing that they're an authorized third-party worker. Understanding how to acquire unauthorized physical access through social engineering is very valuable to a pentester.

Finally, the companies that hire pentesters have their own standards and regulations with which they must comply. Jin's experience with making sure that his HVAC system is regulatory-compliant helps him understand how learning about cybersecurity vulnerabilities can help his pentesting clients with their own compliance. This sort of thinking is also useful when Jin has to make sure that his pentesting work fulfills the legal agreements he makes with the companies that hire him to conduct ethical hacking tasks.

Subject D

Antoni works in a grocery store, saving her pennies for "someday." Her mama has urged her to move out to the country. Or into the city. Wherever, as long as it's not in *her* house. If Antoni wants to live on her own and trade in her Chevy for a Cadillac, perhaps a pentesting career can help her do just that, as there are apparently no good jobs in the town where she lives anymore.

Antoni often works as a cashier, so she understands a little bit about the store's point-of-sale (POS) system. At other times, she works in the rear inventory receiving area, where she helps to unload trucks full of produce, bakery items, or boxes of marshmallow crunch. Once, someone in a van with the word "Dairy" crudely spray-painted on it pretended to be a legitimate supplier in order to attempt to rob the safe where cashiers make deposits from their registers every day. Antoni was too smart to be fooled by that, and she called the police.

At night, when there are no customers in the store, Antoni sometimes stocks shelves and takes inventory. In the daytime, there are occasionally customers who ask for their help in locating certain food items. While some customers are very nice, other customers aren't very nice at all.

So what skills does Antoni have that could be transferable to her pentesting career? You ought to know by now—there are lots of them! As a pentester, Antoni may be working for retailers that have their own POS systems. POS exists both in brick-and-mortar stores and online, and there are standards like PCI-DSS (Payment Card Industry Data Security Standard) with which they must comply. Antoni could be pentesting POS systems to see what vulnerabilities she can find.

One of the objectives of pentesting physical security controls and social engineering is to find vulnerabilities that shady characters pretending to be authorized third parties could exploit, like that fool in the "Dairy" van. Stocking shelves and taking inventory requires attention to detail, as Antoni makes her own inventory of potential vulnerabilities—physical, administrative, and human—in software, hardware, and networking. Dealing with customers requires social skills, patience, and empathy, which is helpful when dealing with pentesting clients and communicating the security vulnerabilities she discovers. Antoni is well on her way toward a satisfying pentesting career.

Skill Gaps

So, whatever your professional background, you likely have at least a few of the skills that could be useful to a career in pentesting. Nonetheless, there will also be all kinds of skills and knowledge that you'll lack, no matter what. There's nothing wrong with that—even the authors of this book learn something new every day about computer technology or life in general. Always be a life-long learner!

It will help you on your journey to becoming a pentester to figure out which skills you lack, so that you can work on developing them. Chapters 2, 3, 4, and 6 explained thoroughly the various skills and knowledge that pentesters are expected to have, so you can use that as your guide to pinpoint what you need to acquire. Table 7.1 is also an excellent starting point for taking stock of your skills and pinpointing any gaps.

While we're here, we should let you know about a matter that people in the cybersecurity industry love to talk about. Both employers and people who work in the industry often talk about a *cybersecurity skills gap*. Employers often say that potential job applicants lack the required skills in the roles that they are trying to fill, whereas people who actually work in the industry talk about how employers look for *unicorns*; that is, people with combinations of skills and experience virtually no one has.

Sometimes, people who work in the industry notice that job postings have impossible requirements like "must have 20 years of experience with Windows Server 2016," so they can find a legal loophole to recruit an offshore job candidate for much lower pay.

Another matter is employers wanting employees to assume the full cost and burden of training. In previous decades, employers were more likely to invest in their employees by covering the cost of training courses and paying employees their wages or salary while they learned to do the work they would begin once they completed their training. Though sometimes employers still invest money and time on training programs, anecdotally fewer do these days.

We implore you to prepare yourself to acquire all of the skills and experience that you'll need to be hired in a pentesting role. Nevertheless, in our opinion, it would be beneficial if more employers would do more to address any apparent "skills gaps" at their own expense. Sometimes, the term "skills gap" can be quite controversial in the cybersecurity industry!

Action Plan

So, you know which skills you already have and which skills you need to work on. It's time to formulate an action plan!

If you've never worked with computers professionally before, you should focus on the general beginner IT skills and certifications that we discussed in Chapter 2. CompTIA A+, Network+, Security+, and Linux+ certifications are very useful to have. They'll give you a foundational understanding of how the computer systems that you'll be pentesting work. You'll also find that having those certifications is useful as you move on to more advanced certifications that are specific to ethical hacking.

While you're at home using your own equipment, give your general IT skills a try. Install operating systems directly onto your own computers or within VMs. Go into your OS settings and try a variety of different configurations. We also recommend that you try installing VMs running server operating systems like Windows Server and Red Hat. There are all kinds of advanced applications there, like Active Directory for administrating Windows clients.

If you have a wired printer, try connecting it to your home LAN through Wi-Fi instead. If your printer is connected through Wi-Fi, try a wired USB connection instead. See if you can get the various computers, peripherals, video game consoles, and Internet of Things devices in your home LAN to work with each other.

If you're moving from another IT role to an ethical hacking career, you can focus on the certifications that are mentioned in Chapter 6, "Certifications and Degrees." The Certified Ethical Hacker, PenTest+, and OSCP certifications are a good to start. Read books, do research online, and enroll in programs that will help you prepare for those certification exams. While you're at it, build a pentesting lab, as described in Chapter 5, "Building a Pentesting Lab." Before you take a single exam, you can practice simulating cyberattacks in virtual machines, in virtual networks, and on your own computers and mobile devices.

As you acquire the various skills that you'll need as a pentester, you'll need to gain experience and find employment. Chapter 8, "Gaining Experience," will describe various ways that you can get experience that will increase your chances of landing a job. Chapter 9, "Getting Employed as a Pentester," has lots of tips for finding employment as a pentester. Not everyone who tries to enter the field has a solid idea of how to do so successfully, so hopefully our tips and what you'll learn from the stories of actual pentesters throughout this book will give you a major advantage!

Summary

As you prepare to work as a pentester, you'll first need to take an inventory of the skills that you already have. You'll be surprised how even jobs outside the computer technology world can offer many transferable skills to an ethical hacking career. For instance, an HVAC technician has an advantage when it comes to testing the physical security of a building to make sure that an adversary can't enter the datacenter by crawling through the ductwork. A retail worker already understands a little bit about the POS systems that they may be testing as an ethical hacker. If you have a background in IT, there are many more obvious transferable skills, such as having a professional understanding of operating systems and computer networking.

Next, you need to work on identifying the skills that you lack. If you haven't worked in IT before, it's especially important to start working on general certifications like the CompTIA A+ and Network+. If you already work in IT and have some of these general certifications, you can start working on those certifications that are specific to pentesting, such as the OSCP and Certified Ethical Hacker certifications. This is also a good time to start building your pentesting lab and trying to simulate cyberattacks on VMs, on your own computers, and on virtual networks.

Now you're ready to move on to Chapter 8, where you'll learn how to acquire the experience that will help you land your first pentesting job!

8 Gaining Experience

One of the hardest things about starting a new career is getting experience. Even entry-level jobs commonly require experience. This chapter will focus on some of the ways that you can get the experience you need to be employed as a pentester.

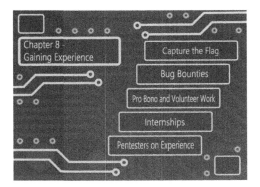

Capture the Flag

Capture the Flag (CTF) competitions are a way to gain ethical hacking experience. CTFs conduct hacking and other challenges that build infosec skills. Some CTFs have a greater focus on hacking, and these are the best options for those who want to be pentesters. CTFs can help you develop hacking skills and the hacker mindset. You can download CTF virtual machines, uploaded by CTF creators, from VulnHub (www.vulnhub.com). You can also find CTFs at conferences and meetups. Following are some great resources for CTFs:

CTFtime: This is a great resource for finding a schedule of CTFs (ctftime.org).

picoCTF: picoCTF is a good resource to check first for finding CTF competitions (picoctf.com).

VulnHub: VulnHub lists VMs that were previously used for CTFs (vulnhub.com).

OverTheWire—Wargames: OverTheWire is a great resource for CTFs, and it offers several CTF competitions that you can try (overthewire.org/wargames).

CTF COMPETITION EXPERIENCES

We asked people who have competed in CTFs about their experiences and what they learned.

Randy

Randy's CTF experiences have helped him gain hacking skills. Here he explains why.

"A significant portion of my childhood education came from home school. As a home schooler, I was used to learning by first trying to solve math problems or complete assignments and then using books or other resources to refer to as I got stuck. Normally, I would do every one of the problems in my math books, and I could be confident that I understood the concept after correcting anything that I got wrong.

When I started going to a traditional school, I remember thinking it was funny to spend time in a math or physics classroom listening to someone talk about the subject before trying to work on any of the problems. I'd often leave the classroom thinking that I understood everything, only to discover as soon as I tried doing the homework problems that I didn't really get it as well as I thought. Doing extra homework problems always taught me more than the classroom instruction.

My first experience with anything like a CTF was NetWars at the end of the SANS 610 Reverse Engineering Malware course. Like most SANS classes, it was a week packed with PowerPoint slides, explanations from an expert, and lab exercises that walked students through each step of analyzing portions of malware samples. I wasn't sure what to expect from NetWars, but as soon as I got past the level-one trivia questions, the value of it was apparent to me. This was the hands-on experiential learning that I needed to really understand and internalize the skills that the class was meant to teach. By starting with real malware files and getting to choose what tools to use, the harder challenges felt very much like a real-life scenario, and the competition gave me motivation to keep struggling with the hard problems.

I made the prideful mistake of not using the hint system at the start, and when the instructor pointed out how there was only one person who had used zero hints halfway through the day, I felt like I had to continue to solve challenges without taking hints.

Now that I have more experience, I understand that hints are an important part of the CTF experience; hints help you get through more challenges in the time available, which means you learn more. Struggling with the challenges for a little while is also an important part of the process to build memory: your mind is more likely to hold onto knowledge when you've worked hard to figure it out for some reason. Maybe because it seems like it must be important. I learned so much from that reverse engineering NetWars that turned out to be very practical and applicable to work later on.

After that first CTF experience, I was hooked! It was like I had discovered a secret to learning skills faster and better than any classroom. It wasn't quite as cool as that scene in The Matrix in which Neo learns Kung Fu instantly, but it sure was fun. I did every CTF that was available, from DEFCON to HushCon and the DoD Cyber-Stakes CTF. Many of these CTFs had challenges in areas that I had zero experience or knowledge. Sometimes, I had to Google the words in the question just to understand what it was even asking. I really loved the challenges involving exploiting vulnerabilities in web-based applications, because I developed software and learned a lot about what NOT to do in my code.

I took many more SANS classes, and in each one I made a point to talk with the other students to ask them if they were going to stick around for the Saturday NetWars session. In every class, *there were a few people who had struggled all week and said they didn't think they could do the team-based class NetWars CTF without bringing their team score down. I made a point to convince them to try, recruiting them to my team with the promise that we wouldn't care about points, and that everyone who figured out any answer would explain the solution and how they figured it to our whole team. Every time I put it that way, the reluctant student agreed to join, and usually one or two others who had been listening in asked to join the team, too. Our little bands of misfits rarely won the coins, but we got something much better: learning together and having a really great time. I usually brought in a bag of candy, cookies, and drinks to share with the team, which made it more like a party.*

When I had a chance to design curriculum for a one-day class on digital forensics, I decided to center the class around a CTF. We spent 80 percent of the class time on the CTF and 20 percent on answering questions to help people with anything they had trouble with. I had everyone work in teams of two with people who self-identified as less experienced working with a more experienced teammate. Almost all the challenges were taken from real cases or incidents that I or my co-instructor had worked on. We provided lots of snacks and drinks and played music (video game theme songs with no words). There was always a small prize for the winning team. The students always rated this class very highly and reported that they learned a lot.

I still think that CTFs are the best way to learn InfoSec skills. I don't think I'll ever get tired of them!"

We can relate to Randy's autodidactic nature because we taught ourselves a lot of infosec skills too! In fact, by reading this book, you're engaging in autodidacticism of your own. Good job!

Justadrawer

Justadrawer discussed two different CTFs they've done: Flare-On and Codebreaker.

"*The very first CTF I did was FireEye's Flare-On challenge. I was currently going through a cybersecurity course and had a background in IT and programming. I wanted to get more hands-on experience in reverse engineering, so I decided to sign up. I had read some books and blogs about assembly languages and reverse engineering, but I never did any before the CTF. I felt the best way to learn was to dive in and see how far I could go. The thing I really like about Flare-On is that it's six weeks long and not just a weekend. This gives you more time to learn as you go and to research what you don't know.*

I completed the first three challenges without much trouble but got stuck on the fourth challenge. I worked on it a few days and was able to get an idea of what it did, but no way to move forward. I ended up asking people questions on Twitter about this problem and they helped to point me in the right direction. The nice thing about everyone I talked to about this CTF is that they're all there to learn and help others.

I continued through the tasks, finding out as much as I could, but usually had to ask for help on each challenge. I wasn't able to complete all the tasks, but with help and a lot of research and hard work, I completed 11 of 12 tasks. I thought it was a good win for my first CTF.

My second CTF was NSA's Codebreaker challenge that they put on annually. Unlike Flare-On, this one ran from September until December and has tasks for more than reverse engineering. The reason this CTF runs so long is because it's geared to college students who may not have as much time to work on a challenge.

This challenge was set up as if you were doing an investigation of a compromised network. The first challenge was identifying compromised systems based on network traffic. The second was to write short rules on failed logins in encrypted traffic. Third was to exploit a vulnerability to log in, based on source code. Fourth was to publish arbitrary messages without authenticating. Fifth was to do memory analysis on a compromised Linux box, extract the binary, and analyze it for information about the attacker's server. The final challenge was to analyze a sample of the attacker's server and build an exploit to cause the server to send a shutdown command to the botnet.

During the challenge, I was able to beat five of the six tasks. I did a lot of research and learned a lot. But what I think I learned the most is not to get set on a possible solution. During the fifth task I made a bad assumption, and this caused me to take longer to find the answer. Even as I reversed the rest of the binary and didn't find anything, I would not change my assumption. I eventually started over and learned something about the tool I was using that I didn't know before. I had made the assumption that my dissembler found all the functions in the code, but it only found the functions that were directly called. The function I was looking for, though, was indirectly called.

Only five or so people were able to finish number six during the challenge. After the challenge, I got a hint on how to move forward and pass the part I was stuck on. I then spent another month figuring out how to exploit the server. It required understanding the Python code enough to understand some of the side effects. I then spent time creating a write up, which I believe was really worth it. It helped me figure out how to explain what I had done and practice writing a technical report. The write up was found by the creators of the challenge and they thought it was well written and they ended up using it instead of writing their own."

Justadrawer's stories highlight the benefits of lengthier CTFs, and also illustrate how you shouldn't be afraid to ask for help—nor to provide help to others. Flexible thinking can also be advantageous!

Justin

Justin explains why he thinks everyone should participate in CTFs. Don't be afraid! You'll make mistakes, but it's all a part of the learning process.

"My first CTF was the NCL or National Cyber League Competition. I actually had a professor reach out to me about joining their team at my college. After getting some more information from him, I found out that my college 'sponsors' students to compete. This simply meant that they paid the fee for me and I was able to say, 'my college sponsored me!' NCL was more of a Jeopardy! style CTF. This was anything from general Open Source Intelligence (OSINT) questions, analyzing packet dumps for specific flags, password cracking, and Wi-Fi Cracking. So, this was a great introductory CTF that taught me a ton of stuff!

After this, I started competing in any CTFs that people shared on Twitter or ones that I came across during my own research. This included the Metasploit CTF, Diana Initiative, and a bunch of others! During this time, I had the opportunity to meet a ton of new people. I started my own Discord server that had around 10 people in it. These included a few CTF pros, some noobs, and some that have never even competed in a CTF before. My whole idea was to meet new people, share experiences, and help each other out during these competitions!

We ended up placing in the top 25 for Metasploit and first place in a few others. From that point on, we began posting in this Discord channel every time a new CTF was discovered.

My overall experience has always been 100 percent positive, and I always recommend that everyone gets involved with a CTF; whether you're a pro or an absolute noob. It's great job experience and a way to meet some amazing and skilled people. There has never been a CTF that didn't teach me at least one thing. Especially when I get stumped, I can reach out to my CTF buddies and they'll explain why something is an answer or why it isn't. The biggest thing is to realize that even if you don't place in the CTF or don't get first place every time, it's always an absolute blast and a great way to legally test and hone your skills.

The biggest realization is to have fun with it. If you're competing and you're not finding a lot of flags and you're getting frustrated, just remember, these are meant to be difficult. If you signed up for the CTF and you're trying, you're heading in the right direction. My recommendation is, if you have a friend or a group of like-minded people, create a CTF team and compete together! I honestly think you'll learn a lot more than just competing by yourself!"

Don't worry about winning a prize in a CTF. The real prize is what you learn along the way. It's not about the destination; it's all about the journey.

John Hammond
John Hammond's experiences inspired him to create his own YouTube channel!

"My stance on CTFs (and I have thought about making a video with this title) is simple: CTFs have changed my life.

I started to move into the cybersecurity scene when I first played a live competition of CyberStakes (which at the time I did not even realize was CTF) put on by the Plaid Parliament of Pwning/ForAllSecure for all the US military service academy cadets back in 2015. That was so much fun, I asked the organizers what I should do to practice and sharpen my skills to get better at this sort of thing and they pointed me towards a ton of resources like ctftime.org, overthewire.org, *SmashTheStack, and lots more.*

I began to train on these 'wargames' and soon started to create practice challenges for my teammates. We would play as many online competitions as we could, and we would even host our own events locally just for our friends to grow and learn more.

Around that time, I started to produce videos on my YouTube channel on Capture the Flag resources, and it slowly started to grow. (Check it out at www.youtube.com/channel/UCVeW9qkBjo3zosnqUbG7CFw.)

After joining forces with some InfoSec content creators in the community, the channel grew from 10,000 to 20,000 to suddenly 40,000, and then now 90,000—looking to break over 100,000 subscribers soon. With that I sort of got on the map in the Capture the Flag and cybersecurity scene. I have started to give talks and presentations at local security conferences, been invited to attend the Google CTF finals in London, have had numerous opportunities open up to me, and I am just so grateful. I owe all the kudos and thank you's to the abundant community and the people within cybersecurity.

Just recently I hosted a virtual security conference with NahamSec (Ben Sadeghipour), The Cyber Mentor (Heath Adams), and STOK (Fredrik Alexandersson)—'NahamCon.' I hosted the CTF competition with challenges that I created, and it was an overwhelming success with over 5,000 registered users. It is so incredibly fulfilling to see the community writeups and seeing people learn (nahamcon.com/).

We did an event similar to this back in April, VirSecCon, where I once again hosted the CTF and our numbers and the positive feedback has doubled. This has laid a great foundation, and now I am working more and more with HackerOne and other big names to provide training.

I recommend Capture the Flag and exercises on wargames like Try-HackMe, HackTheBox, and the SANS Holiday Hack Challenge to anyone that is wanting to learn more and more about cybersecurity. CTFs changed my life, and I think it can do the same for anyone that starts to play and learn."

I think it's great that John Hammond makes YouTube videos and that they've led him to so much success. We hope you're inspired, too.

Bug Bounties

Bug bounties are a great way to get web app pentesting experience because you get to hack web applications in a production environment. Bug bounties are rewards tech companies offer people who find bugs in their software and hardware. By participating in bug bounties, you gain the skills you need to become a pentester, and the experience you gain is helpful in interviews because you can explain how to perform a pentest and use pentesting tools, as well as discuss vulnerabilities, how to exploit them, and how to remediate them. While most bug bounties are for web apps, there are also automotive bug bounties, hardware bug bounties, and IoT bug bounties. Some bug bounty companies also do pentests, and you could get the opportunity to participate in those (bug bounties are basically crowd-sourced pentests). Some companies, like Facebook and Google, host their own bug bounties. Others hire companies to conduct bug bounty programs for them. Most bug bounty companies only require that you simply register a researcher account, but others may require an interview to join.

The following are the most well-known bug bounty companies. These companies manage bug bounties for other companies:

- Bugcrowd (bugcrowd.com)
- Hackerone (hackerone.com)
- Synack (synack.com)

Some bug bounty companies only require researcher account registration, but others offer an interview process.

Many software vendors also have bug bounty programs. They're offered to members of the general public (often anyone) who can find security vulnerabilities and perhaps other sorts of bugs in their applications and are able to demonstrate that they actually exist. You don't have to have certifications or credentials that are relevant to application security testing—you could be a self-taught amateur. Nonetheless, it's important not to break the law by engaging in cyberattacks (as opposed to authorized penetration testing) against applications.

Bugs should ideally be found through the normal use of a program. However, you'll probably want to go through the various features of an application in order to find bugs. Think of how testers who work for Nintendo will make Mario jump up and down a gazillion times on a pipe to test its collision detection. They're not playing the game the way someone normally would, but they're not engaging in cyberattacks either. Alternatively, in many other situations, you may actually have to hack software for bugs, especially firmware. But you must own the device that you're testing (or have permission from its owner) and your software hacking must not harm other people's networks or computer equipment.

Applications with bug bounty programs could be conventional applications that run directly in the operating system;, they could be the operating systems themselves, websites and web applications that run in the web browser, or mobile apps;, or they could even be apps running on IoT devices. The software in a smart car could be subject to a bug bounty program, for instance. Or, it could even be the software running in a router, a home security system, a firewall, or whatever.

A Brief History of Bug Bounty Programs

There is some debate about what the world's first bug bounty program was. Steve Morgan of Cybersecurity Ventures believes that the very first bug bounty program was offered by Hunter & Ready all the way back in 1983! It was for the VRTX embedded operating system, and the winner would receive a Volkswagen Beetle, colloquially known as a "Bug." Or, they could have just accepted the $1,000 prize, which was a lot more money back then!

The first proper bug bounty program launched on October 10, 1995, for the Netscape Navigator 2.0 web browser beta. At the time, Netscape's Matt Horner said:

> By rewarding users for quickly identifying and reporting bugs back to us, this program will encourage an extensive, open review of Netscape Navigator 2.0 and will help us to continue to create products of the highest quality.

Despite the success of the program, bug bounty programs had yet to catch on. The next proper bug bounty program didn't launch until 2002, done for IDefense® Security Intelligence, now part of Accenture (www.accenture.com/us-en/service-idefense-security-intelligence).

We all know that a lot of former Netscape developers and Netscape code went on to Mozilla and the Firefox web browser. By 2004, Mozilla offered its first bug bounty program for the browser with top prizes of $500.

The frequency and availability of bug bounty programs exploded from there, as did the size of the money rewards. Many other developers got into the game, and the amount of money involved grew as well. The largest bug bounty prize available in 2020 is offered by Apple—$200,000 for identifying critical firmware vulnerabilities! So, if you have enough money to live on for a year without needing additional income, you could take the year off to find Apple firmware vulnerabilities, assuming you'll find one that Apple considers worthy of the $200,000 in that time. If you're that confident, do it!

But don't quit your day job to participate in most bug bounties. Typical money rewards are in the $1,000–$10,000 range.

Pro Bono and Volunteer Work

Pro bono and volunteer work are also options for gaining experience. Some nonprofit organizations cannot afford pentests, so this can open up opportunities to get pentesting experience. Schools, churches, and charitable organizations are some organizations to consider.

Even if you're working as a volunteer, you must be extra careful to ensure that you and the party who owns the network that you're testing have a legal agreement about what you're allowed to do and not allowed to do. All pentests work within a legally agreed-upon framework. Otherwise, you're just cyberattacking!

Internships

Internships are often used by college students to get on-the-job experience. Sometimes, they can even turn into a permanent job. Internships can be paid or unpaid, but either way they offer valuable work experience.

If you'd like to do an internship, we strongly recommend searching "pentester internship" on LinkedIn or Google. The last time we checked, lots of search results came up!

If there is a hacker lab or computer science program near where you live, we would also recommend asking about internships within those spaces. Make sure that you have a résumé or CV that describes all of your current computing experience, even if you consider it to be insignificant! Any computing experience is better than none when it comes to looking for work. See Chapter 9, "Getting Employed as a Pentester," for more information about looking for work.

Labs

We can't express strongly enough the importance of having lab experience. Even though the work you do in your lab is not actual work experience, what you learn could be used in interviews or technical assessments that are sometimes part of the interview process. What you learn in a lab environment is transferable to real-world pentesting.

Your lab can even be your own. Chapter 5, "Building a Pentesting Lab," goes into great detail about how to make and use your very own lab.

Pentesters on Experience

It can take years to learn how to be an effective pentester. Studying computer science and information technology in school or for certification exams will only be part of your educational journey. Many professionals say that most of their learning is done on the job—and no books or classes can substitute for hands-on experience.

PENETRATION TESTING EXPERIENCE

Hans Martin talks about how he acquired penetration testing experience before ethical hacking was taught properly in schools.

Hans Martin

"I had to start from scratch after my nine years of school. I had craft training, which is part of Switzerland's educational system. Then I did military service and changed to the police. After an accident at work, I was retrained. Because my hobby was IT, I was retrained in that area. And I am still not sorry to have made that move.

I discovered a passion for hacking with the acoustic coupler and refined it more and more. 20 years ago, nobody talked about pentesting, red team, blue team, or ethical hacking. There were just hackers, and those were the bad guys.

The pentester of today only differs in the names of us 'old' hackers. We both detect security holes and report them to make money.

In the course of my IT career, my three-dimensional thinking has helped me a lot, and in the area of network and IT security even more. I then specialized in pentesting and was able to refine my skills and earn good money by selling security to my customers and then installing it by pointing out the gaps in their infrastructure."

Steve Wilson's journey has been fascinating and extensive.

Steve Wilson

"Formal qualifications and job titles came later, but I've always had an inquisitive mind and a desire to understand how things work by taking them apart. My mother worked in a hospital pathology lab, and I grew up around that place, first visiting when I was a few days old (I was born in the hospital my mother worked in), and spending copious amounts of my childhood hanging around keeping myself entertained whilst waiting for her to finish work. In addition to an interest in the various medical technologies to be found in a pathology lab in the late seventies and early eighties, I was particularly fascinated by the 'museum,' a small room containing numerous jars and tanks with bits of people in them—gaining an early insight into the biological systems that make us up.

I also developed an interest in the criminal investigative aspects of pathology and how doctors would attempt to piece together what had happened based on the aftermath and resultant evidence. At home, I had a keen interest in taking apart old electronics and mechanical toys, though I often had little success at putting them back together again. But I understood that you could start to work out how things worked by disassembling them into the smaller components that made up the whole.

Computing became a hobby, and as was common at the time, we had an 8-bit computer at home that I used primarily for playing games. I wasn't interested in programming at first, until the issue of copyright-protected games came up. That's when I started taking an interest in how software worked to prevent my friends and I from copying the games that were available, since we didn't have the spare money to pay for them. Though my parents wouldn't get me a modem (telephone charges were expensive back then), I eventually became aware of hacking via documentation files that were often traded by people sharing pirated video games.

My plans to become a medical scientist got sidetracked in my teens. I left school and did some college courses, mostly around medical science, but with a tiny amount of computer work in them (mostly databases and a small amount of programming). When it came time to pick what to do at university, I decided to take a software engineering course since I'd found the computer stuff far easier than chemistry, physics, or biology.

In the summer between leaving college and going to university, I worked briefly as a security guard, giving me an early insight into some of the world of physical security. Initially enrolling on a basic two-year course, I did so well in the end-of-first-year exams that they offered to transfer me onto a four-year degree program. It's worth noting at this point that my degree course didn't really cover security at all. We did an amount of safety critical work, but nothing specifically security related. In my second year, we were given access to the Internet, where I started lurking on hacking-related Usenet news groups and reading as much around security and encryption as I could.

I had to work in industry for my third year, and I was lucky enough to get a role working for the Ministry of Defence's Defence Research Agency, a scientific research establishment that worked at the cutting edge of information security and was one of the leading establishments in the United Kingdom to conduct what would these days be recognized as penetration testing, although back then the term 'information warfare' was what graced the door of their office. I didn't work in that department though, so my research and development work was more around the defensive aspects of technology than the offensive side. Though I maintained a keen interest in reading about and studying what the hackers were up to, or at least as much as they openly talked about on the information sources I had access to.

Having finished my degree, I returned to the now renamed Defence Evaluation and Research Agency and continued my defensive work. In addition to research and software development, I also was responsible for administering a small research lab and learned to configure and lock down a range of hardware and software.

After a few years, I was sharing a flat with the person who happened to do marketing for the IT Security Health Check team. By that point, they'd moved away from the 'information warfare' title, since the new one was easier to market to a broader commercial audience than their initial military customers. I found out they were horribly overworked and desperate for people to join to help out. I arranged to go and have a chat to them to find out what the team was all about. Though I recognized the faces involved from various departmental meetings, I had no idea about the specifics of their work. They walked me through the sort of work they did and gave me a copy of the first edition of Hacking Exposed, which still sits on my shelf next to me as I type this. They told me to read it cover-to-cover and come back in a week's time for a formal interview. I went away, read the book, came back and regurgitated a combination of what they'd told me and what I'd read, and was amazed to be offered a job as soon as my current manager could free me up to move.

I started working for them at the very beginning of the year 2000 as a 'security specialist' and started learning the ropes of offensive operations and breaking into computer systems. At this point, I still had no formal security-related qualifications—those came later. My formal degree modules, other than getting my foot in the door with the Ministry of Defence, was mostly irrelevant for my day-to-day work. I think the thing that helped most was my inherent desire to understand how things work and a personal interest in the security side of things. There's no doubt that the skills I'd picked up along the way were helpful, but I'd struggle to pick out a specific course of qualification that was fundamental in my getting the job.

I make the point a lot these days, especially when talking to students, that things are very different now than when I got into this game. I stumbled into it almost by accident, at a time when it was far less well known, and competition was far less fierce. I often struggle when students ask me about career planning since it's not like I planned any of what's happened to me—it's all sort of happened by accident. If I'm honest, I don't have the same passion for it as I did when I was younger. As I've grown, things have changed. When I started, I was effectively getting paid to do my hobby. I used to spend a lot of my free time back then building and running systems and writing code for fun. Whereas now the day job is something that I leave at work when I clock off, having been replaced by other interests.

While there is almost certainly a lot more available these days in terms of information, courses, and qualifications, the level of competition for work has also increased dramatically. I would have jumped at the chance to do an ethical hacking degree back when I was selecting courses. In a lot of ways, I'm glad I'm not trying to break into the industry now. I suspect I probably had a lot easier of a ride than people starting out now."

All of your technical work could be relevant to your career as a pentester, including any programming experience that you may have. Sebastian Mora recalled his experiences.

Sebastian Mora

"Leading up to landing my first internship, I made sure I had an active GitHub to document the projects that I had worked on since high school. Not all of them were flashy or complicated, but it was work I could show.

Surprisingly, the company took interest in automation scripts, such as one to drop a payload from a device that mics a keyboard, as well as some other smart house automation scripts to manage chores. Those were two programs that I hacked together and forgot about. I explained to them that I like tinkering and exploring new tech. I think those side projects helped me the most, as it showed that I could program, and I was passionate about my work.

At the time my pentest knowledge was relatively basic, but it was not a hindrance to my learning. Having or working towards a computer science or tech degree earns you a lot of bonus points, but it's not mandatory."

Martino Dell'Ambrogio

Dell'Ambrogio got experience in old-fashioned ways.

"I knew some CTF (Capture the Flag) competitions were also occurring in my region by the time I was hired for my job the first time. But I only started going there with my newfound relations in the field after the hire—colleagues, competitors, and customers.

Bug bounty programs, as in 'open contracts,' didn't exist then. But I had spent most of my own time in the last 10 years chatting online with a dozen security experts of all kinds, having fun, poking around in thousands of organizations' networks, and having virtual fights with other crews.

These activities halted the moment I met the judge, and I am grateful to him that my criminal record has always been clean, and I was able to resume my most precious hobby as a lawful profession. He even called me a few years ago as a prosecutor to help bring a criminal to justice, which is to this day the work I am most proud of.

I also feel like bug bounty programs today are a blessing for those like me who love to learn by doing. It's a tremendous opportunity to start in the field without committing illicit actions."

You may have tried to work in other areas of information technology and computer science before you considered a career as a pentester. If you find that you're not a good programmer, you may still be a good pentester if you try. Abhinav Khanna has been a pentester for years.

Abhinav Khanna

> "I was in my final year when it dawned upon me that I suck at programming, and I don't have the right mindset to get into the software industry. Then someone told me about cybersecurity. Cybersecurity heavily relies on tools, and other knowledge is not really required. So I joined a cybersecurity training program. It was then I realized this field is not dependent upon tools. It requires one to have knowledge about all the things. The market is open to cybersecurity, and there are going to be a lot opportunities if I keep my head straight.
>
> By the end of that training, I knew that I wanted to be a part of this industry. I have taken up various online courses to learn, but I have not done any certifications as of now. It is still on my bucket list."

Keep an open mind. There are many different paths to becoming a pentester, as Florian Hansemann's story illustrates.

Florian Hansemann

> "IT has always been a passion for me. I only notice this today when friends or their children ask me how you can install Windows. My first operating system was Windows 98, and I was 9 years old when installing it! This was followed by a really deep gamer past.
>
> When I was 18, I wanted to become a submarine commander and joined the German Armed Forces. However, during my aerospace studies, I met my wife and didn't want to go to sea anymore. So, I was put on a random job on land. It was the position of an IT security officer.
>
> My main tasks were conceptual activities and checking the work of the administrators. I quickly got bored, which is why I started to deal with live hacking. After my studies, I found my passion here. I decided to take a part-time job in a small consulting company where I was able to work as a junior pentester for larger customers. Here I quickly won self-confidence and quickly became a team lead. Due to less exciting projects, two years later I decided to start my own business in this area. And since 2018, this has been going very well with many major customers from all industries, like banks and insurance companies."

Matthew Hackling also had a long journey to his destination as a pentester. Now he's mainly a blue teamer.

Matthew Hackling

"I got into cybersecurity through a fairly unusual route. My path started with studying the first three-year bachelor's degree in security delivered by a university, which had a unit or two in computer security. I did a minor in justice studies and took electives in software engineering. All through my degree I learned about computing, worked in desktop support, and read every expensive security book I could find in the library.

Then I worked for an engineering firm as a security consultant on maximum security facilities like prisons and reserve banks. My favorite anecdote from that time was when I got whacked in the head by accident with an M16 by a Ghurka while examining some electronics!

I started penetration testing back in the early 2000s after a stint in security operations at a state government ISP. I was doing Solaris, Windows, firewall, and IDS/IPS management. I was laterally hired in as a client manager into what became the security and privacy team at Deloitte, based on my experience in consulting and security technologies. We started by penetration testing internal audit clients, doing vulnerability scans and adding more services and findings on top. We grew into a tight little team and blossomed doing work for banks with lots of manual web application security assessment.

Over my tenure, we penetration tested three of the four major banks, and penetration tested and audited Internet banking for the banking regulator for two minor banks. We put a few of us through a CISSP bootcamp, which wasn't too hard with all the experience I had already gathered, and the constant learn a new technology the night before testing it routine. An acquisition brought more new colleagues and source code analysis skills.

I remember making a banking system play the theme song from Ghostbusters to illustrate what running arbitrary code meant. I remember a young colleague making a great web application security finding and taking her with me to brief all of the project team *so proud of her achievement. I also remember hard work to the point of delirium, especially the end of calendar year crunch before Christmas.*

Once we worked for a fortnight in a massive football field-sized server room in freezing conditions testing infrastructure. My colleague bled from the nose all over the floor, making the server room look like a crime scene. I have continued to penetration test systems to 'keep my hand in' and 'stay a bit technical,' even though I focus more on building secure systems and uplifting blue team processes these days."

Jean-Marie Bourbon was once a baker who didn't understand much about computers. Now he's a pentester! If you didn't become a computer geek in your adolescence, don't give up on your cybersecurity dreams.

Jean-Marie Bourbon

"I stopped school when I was 14 and started to work in 1997 as a baker. That was my job for 10 years.

As you can guess, I did not do some studies. One day, my ex-wife wanted us to buy a computer to have Internet. It was 2005, and I still was baker. I had my own bakery and was not aware about computing at all. For me it was a strange thing.

I accepted and of course did not want to install an antivirus solution because, you know, nobody would want to target me—I'm not interesting. Few weeks later my computer started to do strange things, and we did not understand what happened! Panic! I contacted one friend to repair it and what he said to me changed my life. Someone can control your computer—it's a Trojan! In my mind, it was revolutionary. How we can do that? I need to learn!

It was the beginning; a passion was born. Every afternoon after one night of hard working in my bakery, instead of resting, I started to learn from technical PDFs, have IRC channels discussions with people, and study how computers are working, programming, how computer memory works, how to create your own program, what a vulnerability is, how to exploit them.

In the same time, I met a community—skilled guys that are here to share knowledge. All the things that disappeared from now, unfortunately. After several years of study and CTFs with my new friends, I divorced. For me, it was time to change my life. I wanted to work within IT security! The problem was . . . how?

I started as developer because I knew programming. By continuing CTFs, I started to extend my relationships that finally permitted me to have my first pentester's role.

Once I became an experienced penetration tester and red teamer, I passed two certifications. But to be honest, even if it was very interesting, I guess that it's not mandatory since penetration testing and red teaming are more about passion. If you're passionate, you'll acquire skills. Specific skills cannot be learned at school."

Summary

There are lots of fun and rewarding ways to acquire ethical hacking experiences without needing to have a paid pentesting job.

Capture the Flag competitions are like the old-fashioned outdoor games where one team tries to capture the opposing team's flag. But the "flag" in a hacking CTF game could be a line of code or a file or some other type of digital object within an application or computer network. Lots of organizations host CTF games in which you can participate, with or without professional experience. You'll learn a lot from those games, and they'll also look good on a résumé and help you make professional networking connections.

Bug bounties are also challenges that you can enjoy, with or without professional experience. Software and device vendors, including a who's who of Silicon Valley, often have bug bounty programs. They're usually open to the general public. If you find security vulnerabilities in their applications and abide by their bug bounty policies, vendors could reward you with thousands of dollars. Some vendors like Apple even offer bounty rewards of over $100,000 if you comply with their very specific criteria and their policies. So, you could help make their products more secure, learn how to pentest applications, and even make some money. If you manage to participate in bug bounty programs to a vendor's satisfaction, it will be good for your pentesting career.

Volunteer work and internships in pentesting can also be useful for your career if you have no professional experience. Just make sure that you have another source of income because these gigs usually don't pay.

You should also assemble and use your own pentesting lab, as described in Chapter 5.

As you can see, there are many opportunities to get pentesting experience before you ever get your first paying job!

9 Getting Employed as a Pentester

The goal of this journey is to be employed as a pentester. In this chapter, we will discuss helpful tips for gaining such employment. These tips are ones that have been shared with students and future pentesters over the years. There are indeed people who have been hired directly into pentesting jobs without prior IT or infosec experience. So, if you prepare well, you can get a job as a pentester without such prior experience.

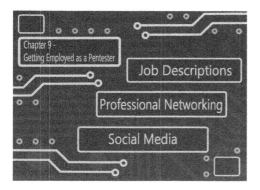

Job Descriptions

"Pentester" and "ethical hacker" are not always listed as a job title. Human Resources uses similar titles across infosec roles as they do for IT roles. Having fewer titles to deal with makes it easier for HR to manage.

Here are some common job titles that may involve pentesting responsibilities:

- Infosec or Security Analyst
- Infosec or Security Engineer
- Infosec or Security Consultant

When looking for pentesting jobs, you must review the job description. The terms "pentesting" or "ethical hacking" will typically be found there. Also look for "pentesting tools," "techniques," and "methodologies" in the job description. Nessus or Nexpose vulnerability scanners and web app pentesting tools like Burp Suite, OWASP ZAP, Web Inspect, and AppScan may also appear within the job description. Knowledge of the OWASP Top 10 Most Critical Application Security Risks is commonly sought, especially in web app pentesting jobs. Pentesting jobs can be found under offensive security, red team, threat and vulnerability management, or vulnerability management positions.

Professional Networking

Professional networking can be helpful in finding a job. Doing this may give you the opportunity to present your résumé to the hiring manager, or at least someone who can get your résumé to the hiring manager or refer you.

Pentesting jobs often come about because of referrals that result from work you've performed on other pentesting jobs. Sometimes, you will need to pass up on pentesting jobs that are offered to you as well for various reasons. People in the security community will often refer people that they know.

Meetup.com (www.meetup.com) is a great place to find infosec-related meetups. These meetups can be educational in addition to being helpful at finding a job. Local DEFCON groups are great meetings for pentesters and aspiring pentesters. OWASP and ISSA chapters also present good networking opportunities.

Industry conferences are another educational and networking opportunity. To get the best results, make sure to talk to other attendees. Some meetings will announce which companies are hiring and also list individuals seeking employment. Be sure take some business cards with you to such meetings and pass them out liberally.

Work on building your social media connections. Social network platforms like LinkedIn and Twitter are great places to connect with infosec professionals and find job opportunities. They are also great ways to learn about tools, events, and educational opportunities.

Social Media

As noted in the previous section, targeted use of social media can be very helpful in finding jobs and for your career in general. Focus on professional social media platforms, especially LinkedIn (www.linkedin.com/feed). Keep your LinkedIn profile up to date, as it is basically an online résumé. You can find many job listings on LinkedIn, and recruiters use it extensively to find qualified candidates for job openings that they are trying to fill.

Twitter (twitter.com/explore) is a good place to learn from and network with infosec people. You can find a lot of good information on Twitter and LinkedIn, including information about industry conferences and webinars. Both are good platforms to find out about new pentesting tools and techniques.

Résumé and Interview Tips

Always make sure that your LinkedIn profile and your résumé mirror each other. When you update your résumé, update your LinkedIn profile and vice versa. Numerous résumé writing services and resources are available, and we will be touching on a few things here that might get overlooked by other resources.

Remember that when you write a résumé, interviewers are bound to ask you questions based the information within it. You need to be truthful and not exaggerate your experience in a certain area or with certain tools. For instance, if you list Burp Suite on your résumé, you should be ready to answer

.... is about Burp Suite. Only list tools and procedures with which you are familiar and have experience.

If the interviewer senses that you are not being honest, they will probe further to gauge your honesty. If you have limited experience, explain your level of experience or knowledge. If you don't have web app pentesting experience, for example, explain what you are doing to acquire that skill.

Also feel free to share your interests. For example, you may want to learn more about wireless pentesting or web app pentesting. Share what you plan to do to educate yourself and tell the interviewer about your home lab. Having a home lab is a sign that you are working to improve your skills and knowledge.

Always prepare thoroughly for interviews. This is important no matter what your level of experience. Brush up on areas where you have limited experience or in some area where you haven't had recent experience.

Questions on the OWASP Top 10 are common, even if it's not for a web app pentesting job. Be prepared to describe the vulnerability, risks posed by the vulnerability, how it can be exploited, and how to remediate it.

PENTESTERS TALK ABOUT GETTING JOBS

Pentesters find jobs in their area of expertise in many different ways. We spoke with some pentesters who have had extensive ethical hacking experience about how they found employment. Their anecdotes may just help you land your first pentesting job!

Sebastian Mora

Sebastian Mora did a lot of work to acquire employment in the pentesting field.

> *"After getting my internship, I mainly was in charge of automating PCI processes such as network scanning and looking for low hanging bugs. I would assist on pentesting or simply just ask my manager if I could spend the day trying to hack something. I ended up hacking into the break room coffee machine and creating a custom drink before I left. I'm not sure if anyone has noticed!*
>
> *To land my next job, I began contributing to opensource tools to help build my GitHub and resume. At the same time, I began actively posting and writing about security on my LinkedIn.*

The three things that helped me the most to land my first real pentest job was my GitHub, LinkedIn, and bug bounties. GitHub shows off your coding skills and any projects you have been working on. They don't always need to be directly related to security. The bug bounties show that you are putting those skills to work and shows the employer that you have knowledge of real-world security applications. My bug bounty reputation is really not that impressive, but I tried. It can be very time consuming on public programs, with little to no reward. Finally, LinkedIn gives you a way to broadcast what you are working on and attract companies. LinkedIn was how I found my current job.

There is no hard-and-fast route to pentesting. I think the main requirement is that you are passionate about security and are willing to learn. Hackers are all tinkers at heart, whether it is creating, fixing, or destroying."

Steve Campbell

Steve Campbell had similar experiences with bug hunting and social networking.

"I did Vulnhub.com *challenges before earning the Offensive Security OSCP and OSWP certifications. After OSCP and OSWP, I worked on learning Burp Suite Pro and learning more about web application penetration testing using the intentionally vulnerable Mutillidae and WebGoat web apps. This led to finding two zero days in the web interface of a popular IoT device and getting CVEs for them.*

During job interviews, nobody seemed to care if I knew how to do buffer overflows, but everyone wanted to know if I knew how to use Burp Suite and hack web applications. So, I spent a great deal of time learning that.

If I had to redo breaking into pentesting today, I'd use Hackthebox.eu and The Cyber Mentor's training, in addition to the OSCP certification. I have also found Pentester Lab Pro to be a good resource for learning web application testing and IppSec's YouTube videos to be a good learning resource.

I landed my last four jobs via LinkedIn and Reddit. I advise everyone to continually build their LinkedIn profile and post links to their blog and GitHub repository to showcase their learning, skills, and passion. It doesn't matter if your blog posts are nothing new and groundbreaking.

When I was breaking into information security, everyone who interviewed me stated that they liked how my blog posts showcased what I was learning and doing in my spare time and was passionate about penetration testing. Your LinkedIn profile, blog, and GitHub repo are extensions of your resume and you should post the links on your resume header."

Steve Wilson

Steve Wilson didn't have much network penetration experience before he landed a job as a pentester.

"Not as such. I read about hacking from an academic point of view, but there just weren't the same opportunities as there are now. There were no CTFs or bug bounties. If you wanted to know what breaking into things was like, you broke into things for real. I have plenty of friends who cut their teeth breaking into real systems, but I was never so bold. I'd go to hacker meetups and conferences and hang out on the public Internet forums that they used, but I never got involved. I was aware of the law, and given my position at work, there was no sense risking the problems that would be caused should I do something wrong and get caught.

Once I'd started working as a penetration tester, things were different. We were very keen on building practice machines and systems and cross-training each other to develop our skills. We had an ongoing challenge in the office—to hack and deface the team's own web server. The only rule being that you weren't allowed to hack it in a way that anyone had hacked it previously, which led to a lot of creative thinking and hardcore vulnerability research and exploit development.

These days, I'm a huge fan of practical security challenges. We get involved in delivering technical challenges often, and I've built and helped with numerous CTF (Capture the Flag) type challenges, both logical and physical. They're great for learning technical tricks, though I occasionally worry that we're building an industry of people who think that CTFs and penetration testing are the same thing.

Bug bounties are a similar thing. As a 'professional' penetration tester, I don't see bug bounties as being the same thing as penetration testing at all. The point of penetration testing is to test for every possible issue and try to identify all of them.

To me, CTFs and bug bounties don't seem to encourage the same level of thoroughness as we need to practice. They seem to be aimed more at 'find a single hole and win.' I'm not saying there aren't transferable skills—there clearly are. But the approach and ethos seems different to me. I still encourage people to get involved with them though, and I think they can be valuable tools when attempting to ascertain someone's interest and skill level."

Wilson talks about which resources or networks have helped him to acquire employment as a pentester.

"To answer this, I again need to bore you with a little bit of history. Back before there were quite so many conferences happening so often, I got involved with and helped run a small gathering of like-minded security folk. We'd arrange the odd meet up, normally in back rooms of pubs, where we'd talk shop and share research and tools we were working on. This was all private and by invitation only.

We grew from a small handful initially, over a number of years, until we had well in excess of a hundred members, including a number of folks from overseas. That seems small now, when large conferences attract thousands of people. But back then, it was sort of a big deal.

As it grew from just friends, to friends of friends, to friends of friends of friends, and so on, I was lucky to meet a lot of like-minded individuals. We shared a common bond of interest in what we did. I'm still friends with a lot of those people today. They've ended up spread far and wide through this huge industry we are now part of. Things were a lot smaller back then! Ultimately, I think that it's true that it's not what you know, but who you know.

When I talk to students these days, I encourage them to get involved in community projects. To volunteer to help run and speak at conferences. To go out and take part in any local security meetups near where they are. Or start their own, if there are none already. I'm always far more impressed by someone who has taken part in an opensource project or the like than someone with purely academic qualifications who has no interest in pursuing the subject outside of their day job.

Also, from a purely personal point of view, it's hugely rewarding to find other people with similar interests to you off whom you can bounce ideas and collaborate on things. Certainly, from my own perspective, it's also a good driver when I might have otherwise been tempted to give up. The past year's efforts to deliver lockpicking workshops and villages at many conferences wouldn't have happened if I'd been trying to do it all on my own. The team of people I have to help push me to be better."

Rachel Tobac

What helped Rachel Tobac acquire employment as a pentester?

"Women in Security and Privacy, the DEFCON community, and the information security community on Twitter are where many of my clients find me. From there it's been word of mouth recommendations from previous clients to their networks! The rest of my clients have found me through my live hacking and social engineering videos with CNN, HBO, Last Week Tonight with John Oliver, NBC, and so on."

When you're in the mainstream media, getting work should be a breeze!

Martin Dell'Ambrogio

Martin Dell'Ambrogio managed to get his foot in the door of the industry without certifications.

"I didn't have any certifications. My college-level apprenticeship degree is in general computer science, and in the end I didn't use the contact that was given to me in 2007.

Since then, I was able to convince my future colleagues and bosses, at the three companies I worked for, of my knowledge and potential in the security industry just by explaining what I was able to do and what I wanted to learn.

What I was able to do was self-acquired in what today we may call the Deep Web and the Dark Web. Although at the time it was IRC networks, botnets, exploit development, DDoS (distributed denial of service) attacks, pranks, and pirated software and movies.

Actually, I remember learning the most during the period I built my first small company. With a friend, we loaned dedicated servers and offered various kinds of web, email, and shell hosting, including IPv6 vanity reverse DNS, TeamSpeak, IRC and other services. They were constantly targeted by young hacking groups that wanted to gain an angle in online games or even just their reputations. I learned how these attacks worked, how to replicate them, and how to defend my infrastructure from them.

Today, it's even easier to build services in the public cloud, and opportunistic attacks are more common than ever. So, I guess that's still a good way to learn. For my small company, I had fun with FreeBSD jails and Linux RBAC patches. Today, it has just shifted to containers and automation, but there is still much hacking to do. From that to a pentesting job, it's a small jump."

Chris Kubecka

Chris Kubecka has done amazing work in cybersecurity so far. She helped protect South Korea from cyberwarfare in 2009. She helped to restore Saudi Aramco's network in the wake of the notorious Shamoon cyberattacks. And she started a cybersecurity firm named HypaSec. Here she describes which resources or networks have helped her to acquire employment as a pentester.

"Friends, mentors, mixed-gender groups, never limit yourself to one group of people. Free or low-cost conferences, military groups.

Doing groundbreaking original research and presenting it. All research I present is on my own acquired collection. I don't present on a topic involving other people's research and act as if it suddenly makes me an expert. This is an important distinction nowadays, where far too many present on a topic to try and establish some sort of expertise but don't put in the work to accomplish the research. If you want to establish yourself, you have to put in the work. Approach it as if you are defending your thesis.

Standing up to cease and desist letters to present research is a danger of pentesters. Good employers will recognize you have guts and can handle any crisis during employment if you stand up for yourself.

There were several reasons why Aramco hired me as a technical executive: demonstrated experience, my vast international network, and so on. It was not an easy decision for a Saudi company and the world's most valuable organization to choose a woman as their first choice. They saw how I stood up to one of the most well-known legal firms, presented my talk with a ghost speaker, handled the press, and gracefully won my lawsuit.

A pentester has to defend findings and have the courage to write them down and present them while not wavering or taking a payout to change a report."

Redvers Davies

Redvers Davies has used his professional connections to find pentesting jobs.

"When one is more than twenty years into a career, one's opportunities typically come from people whom you have worked with before rather than trying to convince an interviewer 'cold' that you have the skills and knowledge required to do the job. All my gigs since have come from people who have worked with me before.

My extended network (mainly from people I have worked with at security conferences) also provides opportunities from time to time, but I have yet to take any of them up.

I recognize that I was incredibly lucky to fall into these positions and have these opportunities. When I'm hiring, I instruct HR never to filter any resumes from us. The best hire that I've ever been lucky enough to be involved with only had one thing on his resume— repairing computers at a mom-and-pop computer store. He was entirely self-taught and ran rings around all the other candidates, including ones with more than 10 years' worth of experience.

I've interviewed hundreds of people.

Skills can be taught. Character, integrity, and curiosity can't. I go out of my way to help good people. I mentor anyone who asks. I was incredibly lucky. I want to help good people be lucky too. I have the best job in the world."

Brian Worthen

Brian Worthen also understands that when it comes to finding work, it's often not about "what you know" but "who you know."

"Network, network, network! My first position was from a friend that became a hiring manager for a red team. I had known him for a couple of years by this point, and he was able to ask around about my background to other mutual friends before he reached out to me about the position. He then brought me in for an interview with the rest of the team and the leadership organization. I passed the interviews and landed the job.

Through networking is also how I got my interview to be a SOC analyst. I had tried for a few years to get into that security company, and I was never able to get them to take a chance on me. Then I had a friend say, 'Hey Brian, I want you to meet a friend of mine. You're both two smart dudes, and I think you should know each other.' Literally, the first time I talked to my friend's friend, I found out he worked at the security company I wanted to work at. Once I told him how hard I had been trying to get into the industry, he asked if I would be okay with him giving me an informal interview on the spot to see if I would be a good fit for a position he knew about. As soon as I said yes, we had a two-hour interview with me sitting in my home office and he was sitting in his car in his driveway. He then told me he thought I would be a good fit as a SOC analyst.

The next day he went to the SOC leadership and said, 'Hey, there's a guy I know that you need to take a look at.' As they say, the rest is history.

I always try to help connect anyone that I mentor if I can. I remember how many years I had to beat on the doors to get into this industry before anyone would take a chance on me. I honestly think as an industry we have a lot more resources for people looking to break into information security than when I started. However, we still have a long way to go."

Summary

Some pentesting jobs have obvious-sounding titles like penetration tester or ethical hacker. Other pentesting jobs have vaguer titles like infosec analyst or security engineer. Be sure to read the job descriptions of available employment offers, rather than just making a judgment based on the job title.

Networking, as in the building of relationships with other people, is one of the best ways to find a pentester job. Go to cybersecurity conferences! Make friends in the computer science department! Find groups of ethical hackers online and make friends with them. You never know where you might get a job. Often getting employed is more about who you know than what you know.

The pentesters interviewed for this book got jobs in many different ways. Sometimes by networking, sometimes by having a job in a different area of information technology and transitioning to a new role, and sometimes through the military. You can often have luck looking online, too. Keep your mind open about how you may find a job, and don't put all of your eggs in one basket!

Appendix: The Pentester Blueprint

To become a pentester, you must understand the technologies and security of the targets that you are and hacking, plus the hacker mindset. These three elements make up the Pentester Blueprint, as seen in the graphic shown here.

The graphics that follow appear throughout the book. They piece together your journey to becoming a pentester.

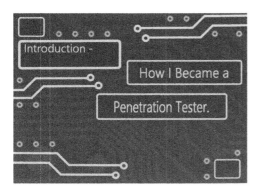

The introduction describes how Phil became a pentester. You can learn pentesting too!

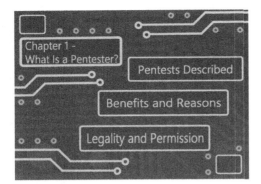

Chapter 1 focuses on what a pentester is. Why are pentests needed? What are the legalities involved?

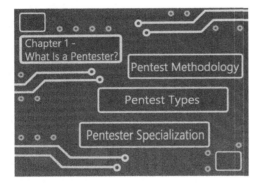

Further on in Chapter 1, we discuss the different types of pentests, methodologies, and specializations.

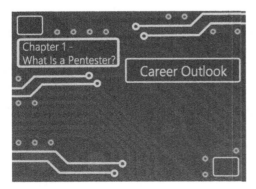

If pentesting is something you'd like to do for a living, what's the career outlook?

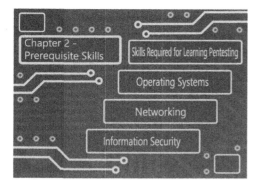

On to Chapter 2! Before you focus on pentesting, you must understand operating systems, networking, and information security.

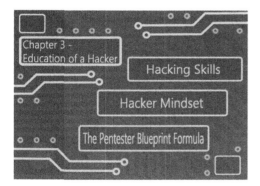

It's time for Chapter 3. Let's examine hacking skills, the hacker mindset, and the Pentester Blueprint Formula.

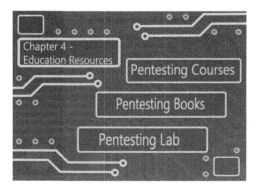

Chapter 4 is about educational resources, including training materials, books, and your pentesting lab!

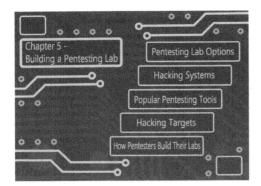

It's time to build your pentesting lab! Let's look at hacking systems and hacking targets.

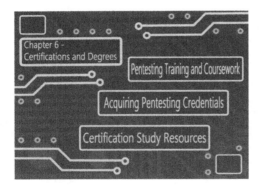

Chapter 6 covers certifications and degrees.

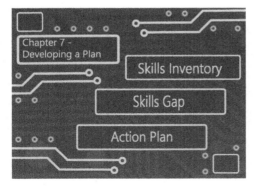

It's time to develop a plan by conducting a skills inventory and gap analysis. Let's formulate your action plan.

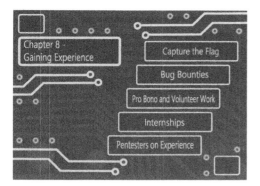

There are lots of ways to gain experience, including CTFs, bug bounty programs, and pro bono and volunteer work.

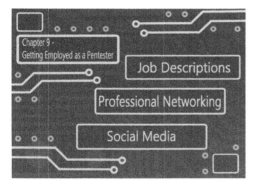

It's time to get employed as a pentester! Let's look at job descriptions, professional networking, and LinkedIn.

Glossary

A

A+   A+ is a CompTIA certification that demonstrates a general understanding of the maintenance of PCs, mobile devices, cloud computing, and operating systems. This is a good choice for someone's first IT certification.

Access control   Access control is a type of security measure used to ensure that only authorized parties have access to applications, hardware, networks, and physical buildings. As methods for accessing data are manifested in many ways, such as through the Internet or on a USB thumb dropped in a public place, access control measures prevent access by unauthorized individuals.

Administrative controls   Administrative controls use company policies to protect security. An example of an administrative control is a policy that permits only IT staff to enter a datacenter, with receptionists and security guards enforcing the policy.

Advanced persistent threat (APT)   An APT is a stealthy and sophisticated cyber threat actor that acquires unauthorized access to a computer network over an extended period of time. An APT could act for months or even years while undetected by its victims. APTs are usually nation-state cyberwarfare groups or advanced organized crime groups.

Advanced Web Attacks and Exploitation (AWAE)   AWAE is a web application penetration testing course offered by Offensive Security to prepare for the Offensive Security Web Expert (OSWE) certification exam.

Airgapped machine   An airgapped machine is designed to have as few cyberattack vectors as possible. They're physically isolated from the Internet, and usually from other networks as well. They often have disabled optical drives and USB ports, and their physical access is heavily restricted as well. An airgapped machine sacrifices usability for the sake of security to a great extent.

Because of how inconvenient they are to use, they're typically only used for working with highly sensitive data.

Availability   Availability is about making sure that data and applications are there whenever they're needed. If a cyberattacker deploys ransomware to maliciously encrypt data, that's an attack on its availability!

B

Black box testing   This is penetration testing from the perspective of an external cyberattacker. An external cyberattacker won't know much about the operating systems, applications, or hardware in a network without engaging in reconnaissance work. A black box ethical hacker needs to simulate what an external cyberattacker would do.

Blue team   The blue team consists of the defensive security specialists within your organization. They focus on areas like security hardening and incident response. The vulnerabilities you discover in your pentesting work may be used by a blue team in order to improve a network's security.

Botnet   A botnet is a network of computers that is infected with "zombie" malware. A cyberattacker uses its command and control server to make the network of infected machines engage in activities such as DDoS attacks and cryptomining.

Bug bounties   Software and hardware companies sometimes offer bug bounty programs, which are usually available to the general public. If people find functionality or security-related bugs in the company's products and abide by their policies, they could be awarded a bug bounty that's often thousands of dollars or more.

C

Capture the Flag (CTF)   Capture the Flag is a fun game for ethical hackers. Something like a line of code or a file is hidden on a computer or in a network, and participants must use their hacking skills in order to find it.

Certified Ethical Hacker (CEH)   The CEH is a certification that's offered by EC-Council. It covers general penetration testing knowledge and skills. This is a good certification to acquire as you begin your ethical hacking career.

Common Vulnerabilities and Exposures (CVE)   The CVE is a large and growing database of security vulnerabilities in all kinds of software, hardware, and networking devices. In fact, most known vulnerabilities end up recorded in the CVE. Anyone can look up information there.

Confidentiality Confidentiality is about making sure that data is only available to authorized parties. If a cyberattacker acquires data that they're not allowed to have, that's a threat to confidentiality.

Cryptography Cryptography is the science of transforming data into unreadable code for the purpose of confidentiality. The computers and networks we use every day implement cryptography in many different ways, but the science actually predates electronic computers!

Cryptominers Cryptominers use a computer's CPU and memory in order to generate cryptocurrency such as Bitcoin or Monero. When they're used with the permission of a computer owner, they're not malicious. But cryptominers used without authorization are definitely malware.

Cyber Kill Chain The Cyber Kill Chain is a model for how cyberattacks by APTs work, step by step. It's inspired from the kill chain concept used in kinetic warfare to determine how a military needs to strike their target.

Cybersecurity skills gap The cybersecurity skills gap is the idea that the workforce lacks necessary cybersecurity skills. This is a controversial topic in the industry. Employers say that the workforce lacks skills. People who work in the industry say that employers are unwilling to invest in training and they often have unrealistic expectations, such as 20 years' experience with five-year-old operating systems.

D

Dark web The dark web is the part of the web that's only accessible through proxy networks such as Tor or I2P. Not everything that's done on the dark web is illicit or illegal. But because of how Tor and I2P anonymize users and servers, the dark web is a preferred means of conducting illegal activity such as selling illicit drugs or planning cyberattacks.

Dark web markets Dark web markets are online stores that only operate on the dark web. They usually follow a model similar to eBay, where anyone can buy or sell goods, and buyers and sellers have usernames with associated reputations. Most of what's sold in a dark web market is illegal, such as illicit drugs or collections of sensitive data breached in cyberattacks.

Discretionary access control (DAC) DAC is a type of access control system that grants access to users according to their identities or the groups to which they belong. Unlike mandatory access control, users in a DAC system may be able to grant certain permissions to other users.

Distributed denial of service (DDoS) attacks   A denial of service attack is when a computer or other such network vector is deliberately sent way more data than it can handle, causing it to go out of service. A distributed denial of service attack is conducted by a large number of computers, often in a botnet.

E

EJPT   EJPT stands for the eLearnSecurity Junior Penetration Tester certification. It's offered by eLearnSecurity to demonstrate penetration testing skills and knowledge at a beginner level.

eLearnSecurity Web Application Penetration Tester (EWPT)   The eLearn-Security Web Application Penetration Tester certification is offered by eLearn-Security to demonstrate general web application pentesting skills and knowledge.

Encryption   Encryption is the application of cryptography. So, cryptographic technology renders data as ciphertext, thus performing the act of encryption.

End user   An end user is a consumer of computer technology, whether in a workplace or at home. The phrase differentiates computer users from the administrators and developers of computer technology.

Endpoint   An endpoint is a PC, mobile device, video game console, or Internet of Things (IoT) device that people use to access applications and networks. The word differentiates computers used for consumption with the servers that provide the endpoints with data and administration.

Ethical hacker   Ethical hacker is another way to describe a penetration tester. So, whereas a malicious hacker is a cyberattacker who causes deliberate harm to computer systems, an ethical hacker simulates cyberattacks with consent, so that security vulnerabilities can be found.

F

Fileless malware   Fileless malware is malware that runs entirely within the memory of its targeted computer, therefore leaving no traces on its hard drive or other data storage. Cyberattackers designed fileless malware to evade detection by antivirus software.

G

GIAC Assessing and Auditing Wireless Networks (GAWN)   The GAWN is a certification offered by GIAC to demonstrate knowledge and skills in pentesting wireless networks, Wi-Fi and WLANs specifically.

GIAC Exploit Researcher and Advanced Penetration Tester (GXPN) The GXPN is an advanced pentesting certification offered by GIAC. Someone with the certification has knowledge and skills in areas such as Python scripting, fuzzing, and cracking encryption.

GIAC Mobile Device Security Analyst (GMOB) The GMOB certification is offered by GIAC to demonstrate knowledge and skills pertaining to pentesting mobile devices such as iPhones and Android phones.

GIAC Penetration Tester (GPEN) The GPEN certification is offered by GIAC to demonstrate general pentesting knowledge and skills.

GIAC Web Application Penetration Tester (GWAPT) The GWAPT certification is offered by GIAC to demonstrate web application pentesting knowledge and skills.

Gray box testing Gray box testing is conducted from a perspective between white box and black box testing. A penetration tester will test a network with knowledge equivalent to a company employee who doesn't work in the IT department.

H

Hacker mindset The hacker mindset is the ability to think like a hacker and be able to find ways to exploit vulnerabilities. The hacker mindset is the culmination of creative and analytical thinking. It's the key focus of this book!

Hacktivists Hacktivists are cyberattackers who are motivated by politics rather than monetary gain. For instance, there's probably no money to be made by defacing a fur retailer's web pages with images of slaughtered animals. So, the attackers are hacktivists who are motivated by their animal rights beliefs.

Honeypot A honeypot is an endpoint or server within a network that's designed to attract cyberattacks. Honeypots are deployed both to keep cyberattacks away from important computers and to analyze cyberattacks.

Hybrid network A hybrid network combines an organization's on-premises network with a cloud service. A hybrid network contains both an organization's own computers and computers that are owned by a cloud provider, with everything operating as one network.

I

I2P I2P is one of the popular proxy networks that anyone may use on their PCs and mobile devices with the right software. One can use most ordinary Internet services through I2P, and also on the parts of the web that are only accessible through the I2P network. While in the network, Internet traffic is anonymized. Websites that can only be accessed through I2P use the .i2p top-level domain.

Incident response Incident response is how organizations respond to cyber incidents. Many organizations have CSIRTs (computer security incident response teams) and incident response policies and procedures.

Industrial control systems (ICS) ICS is a way that computer technology interacts with industrial equipment and machines in places like manufacturing plants and power plants. Therefore, cyberattacks on ICS can be very expensive and dangerous!

Information security Information security is about protecting information in all forms, both digital and analog. All cybersecurity, IT security, and network security is information security. But information security also pertains to protecting information that's written on paper or spoken to people.

Integrity Integrity is all about making sure that data isn't altered without authorization. Adding or removing data in files maliciously is an attack on integrity.

Internet of Things (IoT) The Internet of Things is all about getting things that don't present as traditional computers working with Internet technology. IoT devices can be anything from car audio systems to "smart" refrigerators, from Internet-connected pacemakers to Google Home smart speakers.

K

Kali Linux Kali Linux is an operating system that was designed specifically for penetration testing. It contains hundreds of applications, such as Metasploit Framework, Wireshark, and Nmap. Pretty much all pentesters use Kali Linux these days at times.

Keystroke loggers Keystroke loggers are applications or hardware devices that are designed to record a user's keyboard input. They're often called *keyloggers*. Old-fashioned keyloggers are often physical devices that are plugged in between a keyboard and PC. Most keyloggers these days are malware or software that's deployed to monitor employees.

L

Least privilege The principle of least privilege is a cybersecurity concept that protects applications and data by only granting user access to the parts of computer systems that they need in order for them to do their work.

Linux+   Linux+ is a CompTIA certification that demonstrates skills and knowledge with Linux-based operating systems.

Local area network (LAN)   A LAN is a small computer network that's contained within one physical workplace or home.

Logical controls   Logical controls are security measures protecting data and applications that are designed in the computer systems themselves. Logical controls are often written into software. They manifest in many different ways: from passwords to firewalls, from biometrics to user identities.

M

Malware   Malware is all malicious software. If a file or application is designed to do harm, it's malware.

Mandatory access control (MAC)   MAC is one of the strictest ways to implement access control. A MAC system's security policy is centrally controlled by a security policy administrator. Users do not have the ability to modify permissions or to grant permissions to other users in any way, even when they're the author of a file.

Metropolitan area network (MAN)   A MAN connects LANs within a 5- to 50-kilometer range. They can be deployed within a college or university campus, or by a company with multiple buildings in a town or city.

Mobile Application Security and Penetration Testing (MASPT)   The MASPT certification is offered by eLearnSecurity to demonstrate mobile application pentesting skills and knowledge.

Modular malware   Modular malware contains multiple modules that can perform different kinds of cyberattacks. They start their work by infecting a targeted computer or mobile device. Then they establish a connection to an attacker's command and control server. From there, one module could be spyware, the next could be a malicious cryptominer, and so on.

Multiboot computer   A multiboot computer contains more than one operating system, usually as different partitions on the same hard drive.

N

Network+   Network+ is a CompTIA certification that demonstrates skills and knowledge with computer networking from a vendor-neutral perspective. For instance, Cisco certifications specialize in knowledge of Cisco networking devices, whereas the Network+ covers computer networking in general.

O

Offensive Security Certified Expert (OSCE) The OSCE is a certification that's offered by Offensive Security as a more advanced general pentesting certification. You're required to have the OSCP certification first.

Offensive Security Certified Professional (OSCP) The OSCP is a certification that's offered by Offensive Security to demonstrate general pentesting skills and knowledge. It focuses on the use of Kali Linux, an operating system that Offensive Security develops and maintains.

Offensive Security Web Expert (OSWE) The OSWE is a certification that's offered by Offensive Security to demonstrate web application pentesting skills and knowledge.

Offensive Security Wireless Professional (OSWP) The OSWP is a certification that's offered by Offensive Security to demonstrate pentesting skills and knowledge pertaining to wireless networks (Wi-Fi).

Open Web Application Security Project (OWASP) OWASP is a community that maintains web application security standards and offers various educational programs.

Operating system (OS) An operating system is software that's installed on a computer in order to run applications. Windows, macOS, Linux, Android, and iOS are examples of common operating systems.

OWASP Testing Guide Otherwise known as OWASP's WSTG (web security testing guide), this is a guide to testing the security of web applications offered by OWASP.

P

Packets Packets are how data is divided as it's transmitted through a network. Rather than flowing continuously like water, network data is sent like pages in a book.

Penetration Testing Execution Standard (PTES) PTES is a standard that provides a common language and scope for performing penetration testing. It's designed by a variety of cybersecurity experts including TrustedSec CEO Dave Kennedy, Sunera LLC consultant Steve Tornio, and Tenable Security Lead Vulnerability Research Engineer Carlos Perez.

Pentest methodology Pentest methodology constitutes all of the methods and procedures of penetration testing. It's the deliberate ways that pentesting is done.

Pentest report A pentest report is given to a pentesting client to convey the vulnerabilities and other security-related findings that were discovered during a pentest.

Pentest+ Pentest+ is a certification offered by CompTIA to demonstrate general pentesting skills and knowledge.

Pentesters Pentesters, otherwise known as penetration testers or ethical hackers, engage in penetration testing to see how a cyberattacker could penetrate a particular computer network. Pentesters simulate cyberattacks with the permission of the owners of a computer network.

Pentests Pentests, or penetration tests, are the acts conducted by pentesters to test the security of a particular network. Pentesters pentest to simulate cyberattacks with the permission of the owners of a computer network.

Personal area network (PAN) A PAN is a LAN that's in a person's home. Most households these days use a home router to set up a PAN. A typical PAN could have one or a few PCs, a few videogame consoles, a few mobile devices, and perhaps some IoT devices such as Google Home smart speakers or ecobee thermostats.

Phishing Phishing is the art of cyberattacking by pretending to be a trusted entity to a target. Phishing usually uses text messages, emails, websites, or social media messages. A cyberattacker engaging in phishing may create web pages or emails that look like those that are used by a trusted entity such as a bank or an online service. An example of a phishing attack is a fake Netflix web form designed to maliciously acquire victims' usernames and passwords for the service.

Physical controls Physical controls are security controls manifested in physical things. Doors and physical locks are examples of physical security controls.

Physical pentests Physical pentests test the physical security of a building that contains a network. The objective of a physical pentest is to determine if a cyberattacker can acquire unauthorized physical access to a network, such as breaking into a data center or an office. Physical pentesting can involve anything from trying to break locked doors to crawling through a building's duct work.

Physical security Physical security is how well a building is able to prevent unauthorized physical access. Physical security is assured through physical security controls, such as locked doors and security cameras.

R

Ransomware   Ransomware is malware that's designed to encrypt a computer's files while keeping the decryption key away from the rightful owner of a computer or computer data. A ransom note will appear on the infected computer, urging a victim to send cryptocurrency to the cyberattacker if they want their files to be decrypted.

Red team pentesting   Sometimes, red teams engage in pentesting. When a red team pentests, a dedicated offensive security group within an organization conducts a series of reoccurring ethical hacking campaigns, sometimes to imitate particular cyberattacker groups.

Role-based access control (RBAC)   RBAC is a type of access control system that restricts computer and network access to authorized users according to their roles within an organization or network.

Rootkits   Rootkits are a type of malware that stealthily infects a machine by acquiring "root" or administrative access maliciously within an operating system.

S

Sandboxing   Sandboxing is a way to contain the activities of malware or applications in general from its operating system. For instance, someone may execute a program in a virtual machine to test how it behaves in a safe way before executing it in an operating system that's directly installed on a computer.

Security controls   Security controls are all of the various ways that security measures operate, including physical controls, administrative controls, and logical controls.

Security+   Security+ is a CompTIA certification that demonstrates general cybersecurity skills and knowledge.

SMSishing   SMSishing is otherwise known as SMS phishing. It occurs when SMS text messages are used by cyberattackers to pretend to be trusted entities (such as banks or online services) in order to acquire sensitive information or unauthorized access to computers.

Social engineering   Social engineering are the parts of cyberattacks that involve fooling human beings. Phishing and Trojan malware are examples of social engineering attacks.

Spear phishing   Spear phishing is a phishing attack that is geared toward a specific human target. A cyberattacker could spend time learning about a particular victim and customize their phishing methods to deceive that particular individual.

Spyware   Spyware is malware that spies on its target. Spyware could send a cyberattacker data from a computer that they're not authorized to access or monitor a victim's computer usage.

Statement of work (SOW)   A statement of work is a formal agreement between a pentester and their client. It covers what particular pentesting is supposed to be done, the scope of the testing, and its objectives. Having a SOW is very legally important for both the pentester and their client!

Subdomain   A subdomain is the part of a URL that comes before the main domain name. For instance, in `www.google.com`, "`www`" is the subdomain. In `boots.gothfashion.mt`, "`boots`" is the subdomain.

T

Threat modeling   Threat modeling is a way to understand cyber threats and how they behave while identifying specific methods, likely attack vectors, exploits, and determining which assets a particular cyberattacker wants.

Tor   Tor is one of the popular proxy networks that anyone may use on their PCs and mobile devices with the right software. One can use most ordinary Internet services through Tor, and also the parts of the web that are only accessible through the Tor network. While in the network, Internet traffic is anonymized. Websites that can only be accessed through Tor use the `.onion` top-level domain.

Trojan   A Trojan is a type of malware that pretends to be a file or application that a cyberattacker wants to entice their target to interact with. Trojan malware requires the victim to interact with it in order for it to perform a malicious action. Malware file-binded to a photo of kittens attached to an email, or to a fun free computer game, are examples of Trojans. They're named after the Trojan horse of ancient Greek myth.

Trojan malware   See Trojan.

U

Unicorn   In the context of the supposed cybersecurity skills gap, a unicorn is an imaginary cybersecurity job applicant that has impossible combinations of skills, certifications, and experiences, sometimes while being willing to be paid like a fast food worker. A person with qualifications that would make Bruce Schneier blush while willing to work for minimum wage is a unicorn.

V

Virtual machine (VM)   A virtual machine is a virtualized computer, using a virtualization client such as Oracle VirtualBox or VMWare. A VM runs an operating system as an application within another operating system.

Virus   A virus is a type of malware that replicates itself by modifying other computer programs and inserting its own code.

Vishing   Vishing is also known as voice phishing. It's a way of using telephone calls to impersonate trusted entities in order to acquire sensitive information or unauthorized access to computer networks. An example of vishing is when a cyberattacker phones a receptionist while pretending to be from the IT department, saying that their password is needed because there's been a data breach.

Vulnerability analysis   Vulnerability analysis is a way to understand cyber-security vulnerabilities, how they manifest themselves, and their risks.

Vulnerability scanners   Vulnerability scanners are applications that scan a network for specifically known security vulnerabilities. Examples of popular vulnerability scanning applications include Metasploit Framework, Nessus, and OpenVAS.

W

White box testing   White box testing is a kind of pentesting that's done with extensive prior knowledge of the network being tested. When white box testing, an ethical hacker simulates cyberattacks from the perspective of a knowledgeable internal attacker such as a network administrator.

Wide area network (WAN)   A WAN connects multiple LANs (and possibly MANs) over a large geographic area (greater than 50 kilometers). If an organization has a network that connects their Toronto office with their London and Tokyo offices, that's a WAN. Sometimes the Internet is categorized as a WAN!

Worms   Worms are a type of malware that are transmitted among computers without modifying other files.

Z

Zero-day vulnerability   A zero-day vulnerability is unknown until it's discovered through a cyberattack. For all of the vulnerabilities that we know about, recorded in places like the CVE, imagine how many vulnerabilities we don't know about until it's too late!

Index

Pen Testing SQL Servers with Nmap
blog post, 62
penetration testers. *See* pentesters
Penetration Testing: A Hand-on Introduction to Hacking (Weidman), 56–57
Penetration Testing Essentials (Oriyano), 57
Penetration Testing Execution Standard (PTES), 6
Penetration Testing For Dummies (Shimonski), 57
Penetration Testing Lab (blog), 61–62
Penetration Testing: Security Analysis (ECSA), 58–59
PenTest+ certification, 85
PentestBox, 70–71
Pentester Academy, 56
Pentester Blueprint Formula, 45
PentesterLab, 56
PentesterLab Blog, 63
pentesting labs
about, 60
building, 65–80
for experience, 126
hacking systems, 67–68
method for building, 71–80
options for, 65–67
tools, 68–70
pentests/pentesters/pentesting
about, 1, 3
application pentesting, 11–12
areas for, 45–48
benefits and reasons, 3–5
black box pentesting, 9, 49
books on, 56–60
career outlook for, 14–15
courses for, 55–56
exploitation, 8
generalist pentesting, 11
gray box pentesting, 9, 50
hardware and medical devices, 13
history of, 50–53
industrial control systems (ICS), 12–13
intelligence gathering, 7
Internet of Things (IoT), 12
labs for, 60
legality and permission, 5
methodology of, 5–8
physical, 13
post exploitation, 8
pre-engagement interactions, 7
red team pentesting, 14
reporting, 8
social engineering, 13
targets and specializations, 11–14
threat modeling, 7

transportation, 14
types of, 9–10, 48–50
vulnerability analysis, 7–8
vulnerability assessments, 10–11
vulnerability scanning, 10
white box pentesting, 9, 49–50
permission, for pentesting, 5
personal area network (PAN), pentesting, 47
Pfsense, 67
phishing, 37–38, 47–48
Phishing Windows Credentials blog post, 61
physical controls, 25–26
physical pentesting, 13
physical security, education and, 48
picoCTF, 116
Pinto, Marcus, 102
PoC (proof of concept), 65
post exploitation, in pentest methodology, 8
post-incident activity, 30
pre-engagement interactions, in pentest methodology, 7
pro bono work, 125
professional networking, 138
proof of concept (PoC), 65
Proving Grounds, 71
PTES (Penetration Testing Execution Standard), 6
PTF (Pen Tester Framework), 67
purple team, 2

Q

Qualys, 10
Quizlet CEH v10 StudyFlashcards, 100

R

ransomware, 32
Rapid7, 52
RAT (remote access Trojan), 24
RBAC (role-based access control), 26–27
reconnaissance, in Cyber Kill Chain, 35
red team, 2
red team pentesting, 14
remote access Trojan (RAT), 24
reporting, in pentest methodology, 8
resources
certification study, 99–102
for education, 55–64
websites as, 60–63
résumé tips, 139–140
reverse engineering, 62
Richland College, 55
role-based access control (RBAC), 26–27
rootkits, 33

Made in the USA
Las Vegas, NV
03 December 2022

61041005R00109